THE GOTTESMAN LECTURES

UPPSALA UNIVERSITY

I

PREFACE

In the month of November 1947 I enjoyed one of those wholly unexpected experiences which suddenly raise official duties to a lofty plane and permit you to act as an intermediary in cementing intimate collaboration between your own country and its friends abroad. What happened was that an American citizen, Mr. Håkan Björnström Steffanson, whose spiritual roots have never completely severed connection with their native Swedish soil, approached me with a message from a friend of his who was anxious to present through me in a tangible way, an expression of deep appreciation of Sweden, its King and its people. And so I met for the first time Mr. D. Samuel Gottesman, who for more than a quarter of a century had maintained intimate connections with leading Swedish industrialists and bankers and whose personal contacts obviously had led to a trusting faith in the basic spirit of Swedish democracy. This sympathy had been further enhanced by the acts of mercy performed by the Swedish people and its government during the war, acts which Mr. Gottesman felt had not been fully recognized by the world at large.

To give a concrete form of his appreciation of the humane spirit which he had found at work in the venerable King Gustav V and his people and at the same time promote closer cultural relationship between the United States and Sweden Mr. Gottesman offered a donation of $ 50 000 to Upsala University for the purpose of enabling the university to invite a number of outstanding guest lecturers in the field of the humanities and to have these lectures published. And this donation he liked to be part of the tribute paid King Gustaf on December 8, 1947, the 40th Anniversary date of his peaceful reign.

The offer immediately submitted to Upsala University was gratefully and enthusiastically accepted and already during the spring semester of 1948 the first Gottesman guest lecturer, Professor Stanley T. Williams of Yale University, was at work, effectively carrying out his mission. His Upsala lectures on 19th century American literature form the basis of this volume, which I feel confident will find grateful recipients in wide circles both in Sweden and abroad, to whom new discoveries of creative values, wherever originated, lead to a better understanding of common spiritual kinship. Being the first in the Gottesman series it clarifies in a worthy way the aims of the donor.

New York, March, 1951.

Lennart Nylander.
Consul General of Sweden.

STANLEY T. WILLIAMS

THE BEGINNINGS
OF AMERICAN POETRY
(1620—1855)

THE BEGINNINGS
OF AMERICAN POETRY
(1620–1855)

by

STANLEY T. WILLIAMS

THE GOTTESMAN LECTURES

UPPSALA UNIVERSITY

1948

COOPER SQUARE PUBLISHERS, INC.
NEW YORK
1970

Originally Published 1951
Published 1970 by Cooper Square Publishers, Inc.
59 Fourth Avenue, New York, N. Y. 10003
Standard Book No. 8154-0347-X
Library of Congress Catalog Card No. 75-126380

Printed in the United States of America

TABLE OF CONTENTS

Page

INTRODUCTION 7

CHAPTER I The Poet of Puritanism 11

CHAPTER II The Poet of the Enlightenment 36

CHAPTER III The Poet of Early Romanticism 65

CHAPTER IV The Poet of Philosophic Thought 95

NOTES 124

INTRODUCTION

MODERN American poetry, it may be reasonably argued, attained its franchise in the year 1855, in the publication of Walt Whitman's *Leaves of Grass*. The devotion to "the poet of the future," as he characteristically called himself, of such twentieth century disciples as Stephen Benét and Hart Crane attests his living presence today, both in his craftsmanship and in his mythologies. All but a few of the poems discussed in the present volume antedate this fateful year; our book concerns American poetry prior to the song of the great iconoclast, and thus may be called in a very real sense "The Beginnings of American Poetry." In fact, in 1950, as we complete about a century of what Whitman named "the new forms," this designation is more appropriate than the narrow allocation of the term to colonial verse. In prosody, in æsthetics, in content, and in many other ways, poetry in the United States before 1855 lacked some of the originality, the force, the sense of assurance so characteristic of the verse of 1950. Partly through insistence by a few leaders on European models, partly through the preoccupation of the republic with self-establishment and growth, verse before Whitman suggests a cultural adolescence. Yet in Anne Bradstreet, Philip Freneau, Bryant, Longfellow, Poe, or Emerson (to mention only a few poets) is a long foreground of talent and achievement. The story, from 1620 to 1855, should be told and retold in Europe, as well as in America.

If we consider thoughtfully these two hundred and thirty-five years, the four strands of poetry suggested by the captions of the chapters fall, I think, naturally into place. Although the Poetry of Puritanism fuses imperceptibly into the Poetry of the Enlightenment, the two are distinct entities in our literary history. The Poetry of Early Romanticism might well, of course, include the Poetry of Philosophic Thought. New England Transcendentalism was a Puritan form of romanticism. Nevertheless, the philosophic idealism of Emerson and of the other Concord poets, with its lasting effects upon American poetic theory and practice (one thinks of Emily Dickinson) permits a separation, at least for discussion. Few poets of any stature before 1855 can be reasonably excluded from some one of these four categories. Taken together the four types of writing represent, for our general purposes, the main patterns in this poetry of the young country.

So with European students always in mind, I have tried to explore in limited space certain theories of poetry in each of the four groups and, whenever possible, to suggest the extent of conformity in practice. It is unlikely that these definitions of theory and practice will add materially to existing knowledge now current among American scholars. It is, however, my hope that the principles and aims outlined in this book will guide European inquirers toward a wiser comprehension of our poetry of the past. For without a knowledge of this past who can boast that he understands the present of American poetry? Especially I shall continue to hope that Scandinavian students will strive more and more to appraise American literature historically, and not merely through the stimulating novel or poem of the moment.

In fact, looking back on my months as Visiting Professor of American Literature at Uppsala University as among the happiest of my entire life, I recollect vividly the lectures on poetry,—but not without tinges of regret. These, more than the lectures on the fiction, especially the contemporary fiction, which so excites all Continental students, demanded that effort on the part of both lecturer and listener which probably implied a corresponding need. Swedish housewives know of our electrical appliances and Swedish intellectuals have read William Faulkner and John Steinbeck. Yet few in my audience knew much of the history or of the substance of the major American poets of the past. I felt then and still feel strongly that for a better *rapprochement* between Sweden and the United States, much may be said for an *historical* knowledge of our literature, and perhaps for an intimacy with the poetry discussed in the present volume.

I have, therefore, revised, and, indeed, rewritten this, the first series of Gottesman Lectures, delivered at Uppsala University during the second term of the academic year 1947–1948. I have had in mind European students, but particularly those of Sweden. I have limited the resultant essays to four, all concerned with the history of American poetry, partly because I should like such students to approach our modern experimental verse with this specific background. In addition, I wish to remind them again of the fact that the history of American literature, though short in comparison with that of Sweden, is not without distinction and power. Its story helps to explain, especially in the poetry, the vigor and originality of American writing today.

In conclusion, I wish to express my gratitude to Mr. D. Samuel Gottesman for making these lectures possible; and to Professor Fredrik Berg and Professor S. B. Liljegren for advice concerning their publication. My thanks are due also to Professor Helge Kökeritz; to Miss Dorothy Bridgwater and to Miss Barbara Simison for reading this manuscript; but, most of all, to my students in lecture and seminar who gave me their attention and often their friendship.

STANLEY T. WILLIAMS

Yale University
New Haven, Connecticut
1 May, 1950

CHAPTER I

THE POET OF PURITANISM

THE PRESENT widespread European interest in American litera-
ture does not yet include the colonial poet of the seventeenth cen-
tury. For the casual reader of our prose and poetry there are Wil-
liam Faulkner, Ernest Hemingway,[1] and Robert Frost; for the
student in French or Swedish seminar there are Whitman and
Melville.[2] Although sometimes listed in outlines for university
students,[3] Anne Bradstreet, Michael Wigglesworth, or Edward
Taylor are, on the Continent, still names of little meaning. One
reason is, of course, the obstacle of language; the beginner in Eng-
lish may well quail before Mistress Bradstreet's archaisms or be-
fore such obsolete words as Taylor's "squitchen," "glore," "reech,"
"pillard," or "hone."[4] The true cause, however, lies in America's
own persistent rejection of these early poets. It is hardly the duty
of European students to deny the authoritative assertions of Ameri-
can literary historians that these were the poets of dullness, of
Calvinistic theology, and of intellectual sterility.

Presumably the revolutionary opinion in America towards these
beginners in American poetry will soon have its reflection in
European criticism.[5] It would be a happy incident if this chap-
ter by its summary of these changes in America and by its brief
interpretation of the Puritan Poet hastened ever so little in Europe
a sophisticated interest in, for example, the challenging metaphors
of Edward Taylor. Its purpose, however, is to show the basic place
of the seventeenth century poet, in both theory and practice, in the
long story of American verse from Anne Bradstreet to Emily Dick-
inson. This juxtaposition of these two gifted women is not point-
less. Living almost exactly two centuries apart, they are not unlike
in their use of poetry as a medium for the spiritual life. One under-
stands better "the white nun of Amherst" after an intimacy with

this "Tenth Muse Lately sprung up in America," namely, with Mistress Anne Bradstreet, "a Gentlewoman in those parts."[6] Thus the European student of American poetry should begin not with Whitman, nor with Longfellow, nor even with Philip Freneau, who will appear in our second chapter, but with the Puritan poets of New England.

The revision of opinion in America, to which allusion has just been made, concerning the seventeenth century poets is, of course, part of a general house-cleaning and inventory in the literature of the republic. Among the discoveries of the twentieth century critics were Herman Melville and Emily Dickinson; and it is not surprising that in the remote recesses of our attic treasure hunters stumbled on forgotten poets. Yet the remarkable verse of Edward Taylor, to cite the most spectacular find, merely invigorated a revaluation already well advanced in colonial literature. After 1920 the stereotyped judgments of colonial prose and poetry were eagerly, aggressively re-examined.

New texts were issued; biographies and critical articles qualified and supplemented the inflated, and, on the whole, unperceptive criticism of the famous Moses Coit Tyler;[7] the subject acquired a firm place in university curricula; and some professional scholars dedicated their lives to the interpretation, if not of the literature, of the ideology of the period.[8] A recent and most comprehensive historical survey adds many names, challenges familiar verdicts, and brackets with the re-discovery of Taylor that of such poets as John Saffin or Richard Steere.[9] This particular phase of America's introspection concerning her own culture reached an apogee in the nineteen thirties,[10] and has continued to show more and more critical wisdom. In their study of American literature Europeans should become aware of this new emphasis.

As clear texts, ample biographies, and fresh criticism have rolled back the darkness enveloping Puritan New England, the antiquarian's place has not infrequently been usurped by the literary scholar. The latter now perceives the singular interest of this early poetry. He observes its alliance with the religious absolutes of seventeenth century New England; from one point of view Michael Wigglesworth's *The Day of Doom* is merely rhymed dogma. He studies its connection with the baroque tradition in English poetry.[11] He recognizes its links with the great poetry of the century. Some of these Puritan versifiers were contemporaries of Milton, who at one time, it is said, thought of crossing to the Colony.

How dependent, the scholar asks, was Edward Taylor's ardent muse upon Crashaw, Herbert, or Vaughan?[12] Finally, he sees in these poets, apart from their reflections of their epoch, new intrinsic worth. In reading Anne Bradstreet's poem on the loss of her household goods by fire he responds to its strong emotion, so ennobled by its restraint; it reminds him of certain twentieth century New England poems. He is startled by Edward Taylor's brilliant metaphors of flower and music. He hears the question vigorously argued by university undergraduates: which is better, "God's Determinations" or the "Sacramental Meditations?" In brief, American interest in her early poets is now strongly established.

Make no mistake. Even the most devoted lover of these poets cannot call them writers of genius. No major poet, no single great poem appeared in Puritan New England. To be sure, this revival of their writings uncovers unsuspected virtues and techniques, such as John Wilson's subtle use of the anagram; and it reveals their debts to the thought of the era and to the metaphysical poetry of England. Yet no poem of the first rank! No masterpiece! Our recent discoveries concerning poets of, respectively, the nineteenth and seventeenth centuries differ in this: whereas the posthumous poetry of Emily Dickinson is a priceless addition to the literature of the world, the posthumous poetry of Edward Taylor merely enriches our limited treasures in the verse of seventeenth century New England. Even if we allow for the severities of "anachronistic" criticism,[13] still these are not great poets; they are chilled by the bleakness of the poetic climate and inhibited by the austere Puritan solution of the meaning of life. Theology, a docile and efficient servant in the poetry of Milton, inspiring him to transcendent visions for mankind, becomes in Michael Wigglesworth a nagging master. Theology permits the genuinely poetic opening of *The Day of Doom*:

> Still was the night, Serene and Bright,
> when all Men sleeping lay,[14]

but immediately forces Wigglesworth down, down into the bogs of doctrine.

This enslavement of the muse to religion would in itself stifle poetry of the first order,—a fact more apparent presently in our discussion of the theory of "edification." Poetry in New England was, as has often been said, the handmaiden of religion. For the moment, however, we may speculate on our doctrinal needs as readers of this poetry. How much must we know of election, grace, reprobation, or of the New Covenant to understand *The Day of Doom* or "Sacramental Meditations?" Much, of course, if we are to comprehend it in detail; a knowledge of doctrine helps us to understand the component fibers in this rough, tough fabric. It would be idle to deny that we derive more from Dante if we are conversant with the scholastic ideology behind the *Divine Comedy*, even as we read T. S. Eliot more intelligently if we are familiar with Dante. For the same reason repercussions in the poetry of New England's specific creed are never unimportant. This truth the editor of *The Poetical Works of Edward Taylor* suggests tacitly by his inclusion of a "Glossary" of some fifty terms, from "Apostasy" through "Works of Efficiency."[15] We shall be closer to "God's Determinations" if we recognize the debt of these dialogues to the Puritan gospel of "The Covenant of Grace."

Such intimacies are, of course, basic in the reading of any man of letters, even of the catholic Shakespeare. A knowledge of Calvin and of Ramus is helpful, but an acquaintance with the Christian drama of the fall, the crucifixion, and the resurrection will often suffice. After all, the doctrines lie in broad patterns in the poetry, in a way not true of the polemical prose of the era. Thus we may read on in the poetry, if not happily and with detailed comprehension, at least with interest. We may knit our brows a little at such a doctrinal echo in *The Day of Doom* as the author's disposition of the damned infants,[16] but we continue to read with a general awareness of the intellectual conditioning of the poem. In fact, I attribute some of the present interest in Anne Bradstreet, Michael Wigglesworth, and Edward Taylor among our younger critics not only to the metaphor but also to this stiff texture of ideas, to the density of content, not altogether different from similar qualities in twentieth century poetry. So even if we ignore the learned subtleties of this poetry, we may still feel the strong presence of the Puritan ideology.

We are confronting the fact that the New Englander of the seventeenth century wrote poetry. Although he may have owned no copy of Shakespeare; although he consigned the drama to "the Devil's chappell";[17] although his libraries were in content overwhelmingly theological; although he was preoccupied with the difficulties of this new frontier; still he wrote poetry. When we read in his prose of the horrors of the first and of the later winters, this fact is so staggering that about his angular verse there still lingers a kind of romance; were it ten times worse than it is, we should read it, almost with reverence.

Since, despite all obstacles, inward and outward, he created poetry, the Puritan must sometimes have talked of it. At rare intervals he wrote of it, and though no corporate body of all his aims and ideals in poetry exists, except from syntheses of our own, he left theories of the art of poetry which we may compare profitably with his practice.[18] Perhaps this verse seems, to use a phrase of Emerson's, a "trivial harp," compared with the music of two centuries later. Nevertheless, concerning the instrument of poetry the Puritan cherished convictions. Wigglesworth, for example, believed that his staves were dedicated to God; John Wilson and John Fiske thought the core of a poem its central radiating anagram; and dozens of poets used the medium for elegies or for metrical chronologies of New England's history. Such convictions, however different from each other and from ours of the twentieth century, had a logic of their own, born of the Puritan explanation of life.

* * *

This basic theory, from which flowed most of the Puritan's ideas concerning poetry, was that it must be the dutiful servant of religion.[19] The incorrigible human weakness of building rhymes the Puritan acknowledged, but he sanctified this foible to holy ends, namely the worship or interpretation of God. In conceiving the highest function of poetry to be not profane but holy, he was, it should be observed, in agreement not only with Milton but with other English poets, such as Abraham Cowley or, later, William Cowper.[20] Although a student of the classics, he was suspicious of their secular or pagan allurements and sometimes even of the conventional invocation of the poet to the Muse![21] For the purpose of poetry was to "edify," that is, to reveal to man the glory of God. Other æsthetic was dubious. We shudder a little to think of what he would have felt of the poet in one of our later chapters who frankly defined the aim of poetry to be "pleasure."[22] This purpose would have seemed blasphemous. All the objectives of poetry were subordinate to one, that applied by a friend to Wigglesworth: "to set forth truth and win men's souls to bliss."[23]

Wigglesworth was, indeed, far more than Anne Bradstreet or Edward Taylor, an example of the subservience of the poetic art to religion. In fact, the idea found frequent and definite expression in both his prose and poetry. We see him working hard on a stave of verse as his day's task for the Lord; and in his Commonplace Book for January 29, 1661, he ponders on his primary reason for undertaking *The Day of Doom*:

> I desire [he declares] with all my heart and might to serve my Lord Christ (who is my best and only friend and supporter) in finishing this work which I am preparing for the press, acknowledging that the Lord hath dealt abundantly better with me than I deserve, if he shall accept such a poor piece of service at my hands, and give me leisure to finish it. I delight in his service and glory, and the good of poor souls, though my endeavors this way should rather occasion loss than outward advantage to myself.[24]

In the same temper he dedicates his book not to the Muses, whom he repudiates, but to "Christ the Judge of the World":

> O Dearest Dread, most glorious King,
> I'le of thy justest Judgments sing:
> Do thou my head and heart inspire,
> To Sing aright, as I desire.
> *Thee, thee* alone I'le invocate,
> For I do much abominate
> To call the *Muses* to mine aid:
> Which is th' Unchristian use, and trade
> . . . .
> Oh! guide me by thy sacred Sprite
> So to indite, and so to write,
> That I thine holy Name may praise,
> And teach the Sons of men thy wayes.[25]

Many of these definitions of poetry as the servant of religion occur in verse. Edward Taylor, in his "Prologue" to "God's Determinations," calling himself "a Crumb of Earth," begs God that he may

> . . . . hand a Pen whose moysture doth guild ore
> Eternall Glory with a glorious glore.[26]

What he can say will depend upon God's answer to this prayer:

> I am this Crumb of Dust which is design'd
> To make my Pen unto thy Praise alone.[27]

Sometimes the statement of this theory is contained in prefaces, as in that to the *Bay Psalm Book* (1640), which disclaims the importance of meter, saying: "Gods Altar needs not our pollishings."[28] At other times the reference is incidental, as in Wigglesworth's preliminary lines to *The Day of Doom*, addressed to those who "attended Conscience rather than Elegance, fidelity rather than poetry."[29] Even as late as 1726, in his *Manuductio ad Ministerium*, Cotton Mather, though disapproving of a soul "wholly unpoetical," warns, in the most extended essay of its kind, "Of Poetry and Style," against poetry for its own sake:

> Withhold [he urges] thy throat from thirst. Be not so set upon poetry, as to be always poring on the passionate and measured pages. Let not what should be sauce, rather than food for you, engross all your application. Beware of a boundless and sickly appetite for the reading of the poems which now the rickety nation swarms withal; and let not the Circæan cup intoxicate you.[30]

Possibly, in a concept of poetry as a vessel, so to speak, of the church, these writers opposed symbolically the "Circæan cup" to the cup of our Lord. In any case, the dismissal of the pleasures of Circe, which form a vital episode in Milton's *Comus*, or those of more blessed goddesses, caused grievous lacks in this poetry. In effect, it meant the banishment from verse, in theory if not in practice, of human passion, human comradeship, and the sensuous love of nature. Of all these the Puritans tasted deeply in their lives, despite their absorption in religion. It meant that in practice lyric feeling was to be canalized into a vision of God or into adoration of Christ, as in the poetry of Taylor; that epic imagination was to be concerned only with scenes in the Christian drama, as in *The Day of Doom*; and that descriptive poetry was often to deteriorate into moral debate, as in Anne Bradstreet's dialogue between the flesh and the spirit.[31] Above all, the theory encouraged in the weaker poets a tiresome repetition of Calvinist and Ramist dogma. It demanded of the poet a contemplation of superior beings and ineffable emotions which even the great Milton found difficult to transmute into verse. Such was the impossible goal set for themselves by these first American poets.

A natural consequence of this objective in poetry was the renunciation, at least in principle, of craftmanship for its own sake. Cotton Mather's praise of Michael Wigglesworth's "composures" derived chiefly from their adherence to this aim of "edification"; they were truths dressed up in a *"Plain Meeter."*[32] What Roger Williams asked in connection with prose many of these Puritans would have thought pertinent to poetry: "And yet," he inquired, "is the *Language* plaine? it is the liker *Christs*: Is the composure rude? such was his outward *Beauty*."[33] Style for its own sake was but another vanity in this vain world. Authors of eloquent but simple prose, these American Puritans would not be concerned with what one of their descendants, in fact a poet in their own tradition, called the tinkling "piano strings" of verse.[34] A few concessions were made to poetic techniques, among these to the anagram (to be discussed in a moment) and to the quality of rhyme. For in verse, even in bad verse, the truths of God were sharpened. Some rhymes stuck like burrs; the jingles of *The New England Primer*, memorized in childhood, clung throughout life. Probably this motive had its part in Wigglesworth's selection for *The Day of Doom* of its swift-moving, incongruous ballad measure.

This mild deference to techniques hardly modified the inner principle of "edification." This principle and that of a *"Plain Meeter"* were inherent in the Puritan's theory of poetry. These ideas were implicit though seldom defined. Had critical treatises been written they would have explained, logically enough, another phase of "edification," namely, the coexistence with the *"Plain Meeter"* of classical learning, and of such "ingenuities" as the anagram, the acrostic, the conceit, and the pun. These Puritans were children of the Renaissance; their intimate knowledge of the Greek and Latin classics rebukes our more shallow acquaintance with these masterpieces.

Thus a plain style might include, with proper emphasis, allusions to the classics, not only in prose but in poetry. A poet might "mingle a great deal of *Mythology* with the Truth"[35] if the truth remained paramount. Learning could serve the glory of God; so, too, could the humble anagram at the same time that it delighted the intellect: "There is," remarked Cotton Mather, "a certain little *Sport of Wit*, in *Anagrammatizing* the *Names* of Men."[36] Mather traces these antics to the Old Testament, but the practice was in debt also to George Herbert and other metaphysical poets with whom the Puritans were familiar. Poetry's learning and its "wit" were not inconsistent with its dominant purpose of "edification." Indeed, Cotton Mather declared that the anagram "afforded Reflections very *Monitory.*"[37]

Underlying, then, this official aim of "edification" was a distinct pattern of poetic theory, imperfectly expressed. Its roots lay partly in the baroque tradition,[38] and to this we may ascribe on occasion the condensation in line, the harshness, the audacious figures of speech, the paradox, or the antithesis of the learned and the homely. The Puritan poet was in debt not only to English baroque poetry but, as has been pointed out recently, to the Continental pietist poets.[39] Although no attempt is made in this short chapter to distinguish in chronology either between the early and later poets or between the varying stages of the baroque tradition in America, we should recognize its presence as a conditioning attitude.

In the many hostile criticisms of the Puritan poet, the premise has invariably been that his verse should have been clear, smooth-flowing, and euphonious. It should be remembered that the seventeenth century Puritan would have held such criteria preposterous. He worshipped other poetic gods, for example, the anagram in which he attained such skill. Actually, there seems to have been rivalry both in the power to "edify" and in the use of these ingenious devices, such as the anagram. John Fiske's anagrams were famous among his contemporaries, and the humorous Nathaniel Ward, "The Simple Cobler of Aggawam," has left us this precious, ironic compliment, lately discovered, to John Wilson's agility in the art:

> We poor Aggawams
> are so stiff in the hams
> that we cannot make Anagrams,
> But Mr John Wilson
> the great Epigrammatist
> Can let out an Anagram
> even as he list.[40]

Remembering always that this brief synthesis of Puritan poetic theory is assembled from comments here and there or even from inferences apparent within the poetry itself, we might add other tenets, all of which are in the end related to the belief that poetry's only excuse for being was in its consecration to God. We are conscious, for example, of the tendency to analogy: Old Testament experiences become in the poetry of Taylor proleptic of those of the New. Joseph anticipates Christ; or he becomes a judge or advocate. Or, prophetic of future techniques in American poetry, the phenomena of nature correlate men's moral history.

Thus in the poetry the correspondence is set up between the drama of nature and that of Christianity. A sunset suggests the blood of the crucifixion, and fruits and flowers take on meaning in terms of the adoration of Christ. So Edward Taylor writes:

> None Eye e're saw, nor nose e're smelt such Fruits,
> My Lord, as thine, Thou Tree of Life in 'ts blow.
> Thou Rose of Sharon, Vallies Lilly true,
> Thy Fruits most sweet and glorious ever grew.[41]

The study of such analogies deepened until we read without surprise two centuries later the words of Emerson: "Words are signs of natural facts. . . . Particular natural facts are symbols of particular spiritual facts."[42] Most of all, analogy was effective in the enclosure of the spiritual fact in the homespun images of Puritan life. Taylor's metaphors include a cask, a wagon, or a wardrobe.

*　　*　　*

Therefore, without giving much conscious thought to poetry as an art in itself, the New Englander must have had in mind some such patterns as he sat down to his "composures." He must "edify." To accomplish this he might use doctrine, a "plain style," classical learning, or the devices sanctioned by the baroque tradition. His forms, like his theories, were more various than at first appear: the ode, the hymn, the funeral elegy, the satire, the verse dialogue, the rhymed history, or the lyric. His was a lonely task: libraries were scarce and limited in content; and the existence of a literary group was undreamed of. At the far-off post of Westfield, Massachusetts, Edward Taylor sealed his verses with the request to his heirs that they should not be published.

Yet the poets were, in proportion to the numbers of the population, not few; a recent critic lists or discusses one hundred and seventy-four who were writing before 1701.[43] John Wilson, Benjamin Tompson, or Anne Bradstreet might in their day be called "popular" poets; and, if to move and persuade be a function of poetry, no American poem has ever cut more deeply into the contemporary mind than Wigglesworth's *The Day of Doom*.[44] Moreover, at this moment every one of these poets attracts the specialist for rare and stimulating variations of the patterns we have discussed; and for the European student at least a dozen are essential if he is to attain perspective in the history of American poetry.

The European student, in whom we are particularly interested, can clarify his notions concerning the beginnings of American poetry by reading this dozen, and by observing how, at least for the present, three have emerged as the vigorous classics of their era, namely, Anne Bradstreet, Michael Wigglesworth, and Edward Taylor. These three will deserve his especial scrutiny, but let him spend passing hours upon the others. Let him commence with the first volume published in the colonies, the *Bay Psalm Book*, and end with Mather Byles, who lived on until 1788 and who rejoiced in other fashions. Within this century and a half the change is definite, from a painfully literal practice of these Puritan theories to those sponsored by John Dryden and Alexander Pope.

In both techniques and tone, for example, Byles's poem, "An Hymn to Christ," is much nearer our own time:

> To Thee, my Lord, I lift the Song,
> Awake, my tuneful Pow'rs:
> In constant Praise my grateful Tongue
> Shall fill my foll'wing Hours.[45]

Eloquent, correct, and genteelly devout, the lines symbolize the change in the poetic temper which had occurred since Edward Taylor invoked his Savior:

> Oh! that thy love might overflow my Heart!
>   To fire the same with Love: for Love I would.
> But oh! my streight'ned Breast! my Lifeless Sparke!
>   My Fireless Flame! What Chilly Love, and Cold?
>   In measure small! In Manner Chilly! See!
> Lord, blow the Coal: Thy Love Enflame in mee.[46]

In addition, the European student may, by sampling these various writers, comprehend the uses made of ode, satire, elegy, and other forms. He should, then, against this general background study the verse of this unusual trio.

The *Bay Psalm Book* was indeed a terrifying realization of the Puritan theories of poetry; this famous volume was a grotesque, literal translation from the Hebrew, by Thomas Weld, John Eliot, and Richard Mather. These eminent ministers, bent on "edification," avoided successfully the inherent beauty of the original, and Cotton Mather was constrained to remark in the *Magnalia* that "It was thought that a little more of Art was to be employ'd upon the verses."[47] This fault, that this particular altar of God did need some "pollishings," did not lessen the enormous vogue of the book. The first edition of the *Bay Psalm Book* numbered seventeen hundred copies,[48] and it was printed again and again. Reading it today, with some discomfort of mind, we still respect the rigor of its adherence to the principle of "edification" even if we find elusive the boasted "sweetnes of the verse":[49]

> The Lord to mee a shepheard is, want therefore
>   shall not I.
> Hee in the folds of tender-grasse, doth cause mee
>   downe to lie.[50]

Browsing still further among these Puritan poets of the seventeenth century, the European reader will encounter poems more secular in character, among them John Wilson's *A Song of Deliverance*, a rhymed record of the Armada, the plague, and the Gunpowder Plot.[51] The title of the poem, as well as the repeated allusions to divine beings, suggests that in this poem, too, the aim of this beloved minister was, even in his dogtrot meter, to "edify." Yet the total impression remains that of a rough-and-ready narrative of sea fight, pestilence, and Papist:

> They fled with shame, the way they came,
>   one from another scattred:
> Their Shipping tall with Cannon ball,
>   was soundly beat and battred.[52]

Meanwhile, Wilson's fame among his contemporaries increased through his devastating power over the anagram; he once concocted six out of a single name! Cotton Mather's admiration of Wilson's talent in this regard was ardent, if somewhat inhibited; by principle he was forced to consider it a lesser virtue. Yet he was unable to conceal his delight in Wilson's

> . . . Care to guide his *Flock*, and feed his *Lambs*,
>   By, *Words*, *Works*, *Prayers*, *Psalms*, *Alms*, and *Anagrams*.[53]

Anagrams were dear to the authors of elegiac verse. An immersion in these, especially in the lesser elegists, begets sympathy with Benjamin Franklin, an eighteenth century deist, who was passing weary of this merciless piety. One is tempted to share his mood as he wrote his famous "Receipt to Make a New England Funeral Elegy," which runs in part:

> Having chose the Person, take all his Virtues, Excellencies, &c. and if he have not enough, you may borrow some to make up a sufficient Quantity: To these add his last Words, dying Expressions, &c. if they are to be had; mix all these together, and be sure you strain them well. Then season all with a Handful or two of Melancholly Expressions, such as *Dreadful, Deadly, cruel cold Death, unhappy Fate, weeping Eyes,* &c. Have mixed all these Ingredients well, put them into the empty Scull of some *young Harvard;* (but in Case you have ne'er a One at Hand, you may use your own.)[54]

Nevertheless, about some of these ragged, stumbling funereal pieces there is a touching simplicity and pathos. John Norton's sorrow for Anne Bradstreet is unaffected,[55] and Edward Johnson's epitaph on his young friend, Roger Harlackenden, is grief militant:

> Harlackenden,
> Among these men
> Of note Christ hath thee seated:
> In warlike way
> Christ thee aray
> With zeal, and love well heated.[56]

A similar passion animates Johnson's invocation to the New England Churches:

> Thou Sister young, Christ is to thee a wall
> Of flaming fire, to hurt thee none may come,
> In slipp'ry paths and dark wayes shall they fall,
> His Angels might shall chase their countless sum.
> Thy Shepheard with full cups and table spread,
> Before thy foes in Wilderness thee feeds,
> Increasing thy young lambs in bosom bred,
> Of Churches by his wonder-working deeds.[57]

Benjamin Tompson, also famous for his satire, adapts the elegy to a chant of the "funeral ashes," or the decline of the colony, in *New Englands Crisis.*[58] Yet perhaps the real rejoinder to Franklin's cool contempt for this *genre* or to our own twentieth century condescension, may be found in the pulsating emotion of Urian Oakes's fifty-two stanza elegy upon the death of Thomas Shepard. The meter is rough; the figures of speech conventional; but the grief is sincere. The poet concludes:

> My Dearest, Inmost, Bosome-Friend, is Gone!
> Gone is my sweet Companion, Soul's Delight!
> Now in an Huddling Croud I'm all alone,
> And almost could bid all the World *Goodnight:*
>   Blest be my Rock! God lives: Oh let him be,
>   As He is, so All in All to me.
>
>   The Bereaved, Sorrowful
>   *Urian Oakes.*[59]

Elegy was not all. Contrary to persistent prejudices concerning this early poetry, within the types acceptable to the Puritans may be found a considerable variety. Reading on, we encounter writings so diverse as the satire of Nathaniel Ward or of William Morrell; the Latin couplets of Charles Chauncy; the historical or topographical poems of William Bradford; the pagan drinking songs of Thomas Morton (a renegade outside the Puritan tradition); the almanac verse of Samuel Danforth; or the meditations on human frailty of Philip Pain.[60] Thus the list of poets is formidable. Some of them linger on into the eighteenth century, sharing, of course, the freer standards of this more liberal age. An occasional love song, such as John Saffin's or a lyric on the simple, humble Puritan daily life, such as Anne Bradstreet's, modifies—let us be thankful—the assumptions of "edification," of the anagram, or of the baroque tradition. Fortunately poets, too, cannot always live up to their theories. In the main, however, the principles discussed in this chapter laid an inexorable hand upon poetic performance in this American verse of the seventeenth century.

So let the European student wander among these poets, restricted in their concepts of verse, unhappily devoid of the genius of their English contemporaries, but occasionally striking fire. The experience is stimulating if he reads bravely on, adapting the moral of a later New England poet:

> Seeing only what is fair,
> Sipping only what is sweet,
>
> . . . .
>
> Leave the chaff, and take the wheat.[61]

Alas! chaff is plentiful, even in the three emergent poets. The best that can be said is that in these the wheat is more abundant than in the others. Anne Bradstreet's poetry is unlikely, as a contemporary boasted, to outlast "the stateliest marbles,"[62] and even Hawthorne's understanding picture of the Puritan family reading together at their fireside *The Day of Doom* cannot remove the Calvinistic blight from the poetry of Wigglesworth. About the distinction of the most arresting stanzas there is a kind of relativity of value: Anne Bradstreet's poetry excels in its tender directness; Wigglesworth's in its mood of terror; Taylor's in its play upon the five senses. The recent discovery and publication of the manuscripts of this last-named poet have added stature to the achievements of all three.

*   *   *

Of the three poets, the two ministers and the frontier wife (the daughter of one Puritan governor and the wife of another), Anne Bradstreet is the most vividly remembered as a person. Michael Wigglesworth, the "little feeble shadow of a man,"[63] the gentle pastor of Malden, is nearly forgotten save as the author of his sulphurous gospel in verse; and Edward Taylor, for fifty-eight years a parson in western Massachusetts is, on the whole, dim, except for his years at Harvard. Yet Mistress Bradstreet survives not only as a poetess but as a woman; she has inspired affectionate tributes down through the centuries, from Cotton Mather or Nathaniel Ward to the latest anthologist who rediscovers her charming poem, "To My Dear and Loving Husband."[64] In this continuing sense of her reality as an individual is perhaps evidence of the dynamism of her poetry, for we actually know extremely little about her. No portrait of her exists; no precise record of her birth; no hint of her last resting-place. Yet we see her plainly. She stands sadly before her household belongings ravaged by fire; or she talks joyfully of her "eight birds hatched in one nest."[65] Like Emily Dickinson (once more), the woman as well as the poetess belongs to us all. Through her writings shines her serene and thoughtful spirit.

What we do know endears her still more: her cultivation of mind; her heroism as "a frontierswoman"; her humor. Various writers, among them Hawthorne, have been fascinated by the contrast between the middle years of these brave pioneer women in Massachusetts and their girlhoods in civilized England. Until the age of sixteen, when she gave herself for the remainder of her life to the "loving and grave companionship"[66] of her husband, Simon Bradstreet, Anne Dudley had lived at Tattershall Castle, where her father was steward for the Earl of Lincoln. Two years later she was on board the *Arabella*, with husband and father, destined to a life of forty-two years on the bleak American strand. In the farmhouse, not far from the Merrimack River, in North Andover, Massachusetts, her heart, which had been at first rebellious at her lot, found happiness in her sons and daughters, in her husband's career, and, despite moods of skepticism, in faith in God. Neither illness nor childbearing nor the wilderness could shake Mistress Bradstreet's moral or intellectual stamina.

Anne Bradstreet's intellectual life was nourished partly on her husband's library of sixty volumes. She read, of course, steadily in the Bible, and, among other poets, in Quarles, Wither, Sidney, Spenser, and also in the admired Du Bartas. In his playful lines "On Mrs. Bradstreet's Tenth Muse," Nathaniel Ward announced that

> The Auth'resse was a right *Du Bartas* Girle.[67]

In some ways this was true. *The Tenth Muse* lay, through the translations of Joshua Sylvester, under the spell of *La Semaine* and *La Seconde Semaine*. Du Bartas helped to persuade Milton to his grand theme of heaven and hell, and also this provincial poetess to hers of "The Four Monarchies." In turning poets to the Bible, Du Bartas seems to have directed some of the glory of Protestantism into the literature of his time. Drayton, Daniel, Sidney, Spenser,— all hailed his poem, which reached its full influence in the reign of James I. Looking out from her home in Newtown or in Ipswich at a countryside which was not to enjoy recognition in our poetry until the nineteenth century, Mistress Bradstreet beheld instead, in her imagination, the world created by fifteenth and sixteenth century minds. For, like some of her New England descendants, she was in her early years a bookish poet. She seems to surpass both Wigglesworth and Taylor in the breadth of her intellectual interests.

Thus *The Tenth Muse Lately sprung up in America*, so christened without her knowledge by the friend who published it for her in

London, was imitative. Indeed, it has been said that not one section under its expansive title of some eighty words, such as "The Four Elements," "The Four Seasons," or "The Four Monarchies" could now interest anyone except the antiquarian. This is poetry fashioned by a young Englishwoman, reading Du Bartas, and striving to escape in dreams of the Old World the rawness of the New. Not yet forty at the time of her book's appearance, she had still to realize wherein lay her richest vein of poetry, namely, in her own humble experiences in the colony. At the same time this early book is not destitute of her own quality. In "Spring" the bird is the nightingale, the flower is the primrose, and the "cleanly Huswifes Dary" might be in Lincolnshire. Yet a passage here and there foretells the more acclimated Anne Bradstreet even if the setting is not indubitably that of Massachusetts:

> The fearful bird his little house now builds
> In trees and walls, in cities and in fields;
> The outside strong, the inside warm and neat—
> A natural artificer complete.
> . . . .
> Now swarms the busy, witty, honey-bee,
> Whose praise deserves a page from more than me.[68]

This playful vein in Anne Bradstreet is never, I think, tedious. It is, on the contrary, beautiful especially when it deepens into the tenderness of the lyrics on her children and husband; and it raises the second volume (published posthumously in 1878) above the mannered first: *Several Poems Compiled . . . By a Gentlewoman in New England . . . Corrected by the Author*. This latter collection contains these lyrics and also her "Contemplations." Her dismay at the bad proof reading of *The Tenth Muse* she commemorated in verse:

> At thy return my blushing was not small
> My rambling brat—in print—should mother call.[69]

Having banished Du Bartas, she now gave herself to a simpler, fresher concept of poetry. More than twenty years had passed; some of her children had grown up; she had borne her part in the growth of the Colony. Though Philomel and classic pastoral scenes still crowded her mind, these proved to be, after all, merely embroidery on the strong, rich experiences of her own life in America. "To My Dear and Loving Husband," she writes:

> If ever two were one, then surely we;
> If ever man were loved by wife, then thee;
> If ever wife was happy in a man,
> Compare with me, ye women, if you can.[70]

The warm, human lines seem to snap the chains of current poetic theory; for the moment seventeenth century American verse ceases to be the prisoner of religion. Nevertheless, in the corrected and amended volume is still heard the sigh of the penitent! In "Contemplations," also, the referents are always the invisible landscape and God. The poetess calls herself a

> . . . sinful creature, frail and vain,
>   This lump of wretchedness, of sin and sorrow,
> This weather-beaten vessel racked with pain.[71]

Here is the dialogue, "The Flesh and the Spirit," with the former a predestined loser; and here are the classical allusions; and, though, less elaborate than John Wilson's, here are the ingenuities and analogies.

Thus Anne Bradstreet did not throw off the garment of her age. What she did was occasionally to disengage practice from theory by using in her poetry the everyday stuff of her life in New England. Joy pulsates through her verses on her marriage, and sorrow in those on the loss of her house. We see her again, surveying with downcast eyes the ruins which had been her home:

> Here stood that trunk, and there that chest;
> There lay that store I counted best;
> My pleasant things in ashes lie,
> And them behold no more shall I.
> Under thy roof no guest shall sit,
> Nor at thy table eat a bit.[72]

So Anne Bradstreet learned in New England the poetry of these common things. Civilized in mind and robust in spirit, she sang from the inwardness of her religious life:

> The hidden manna I do eat,
> The word of life it is my meat.[73]

*   *   *

Yet even as Anne Bradstreet composed these simple lines of faith, Michael Wigglesworth was, perhaps, preparing his hideous objectification of the Puritan conscience in *The Day of Doom*. It appeared, to shock and thrill all New England, twelve years after *The Tenth Muse* and ten before Anne Bradstreet's death. Looking behind, for a moment, this primitive epic of the Last Judgment and the less known *Meat Out of the Eater*, we find ourselves in the presence of a personality different from Anne Bradstreet's and at variance with the tone of the poet's jeremiads. Wigglesworth is discovered to be so gentle, so sensitive in conscience, so devoted in his human affections that his terrible poem acquires a fresh terror from its very impersonality, as if, indeed, Truth itself spoke. Whatever the kindly emotions of the human being, these facts about eternity were, the Puritan leaders believed, as sure as mathematics.

Apparently Wigglesworth had his first vision of his Day as early as 1653, almost a decade before the publication of his poem; at that time he was aroused "to follow God with tears and cries."[74] The experience was typical of his emotional acceptance of the legalistic doctrines of Calvin; Anne Bradstreet was troubled by misgivings concerning their truth; Wigglesworth by dreams of their terrors. His life seems to have been dedicated either to study of the Calvinistic ideology or to its effect upon his own conscience. Yet he found time to be educated at Harvard, to teach there, to become a Fellow of that institution, and to reject the office of President. That he was respected and beloved is attested by Cotton Mather's funeral sermon in his memory.[75]

The terrifying vision, which occurred two years before his appointment as minister at Malden, was the culmination of his excessive moral sensitivity, so evident in his relations with his pupils at Harvard; it also marked the commencement of the protracted ill-health which harassed him for many years. He must have written *The Day of Doom* during the first seven years of the Malden pastorate; evidently when he could not preach, the manuscript of the poem became his refuge. In a touching preface, "To the Christian Reader," he says that his suffering had lasted for ten years. A "Prisoner, Under a heavy Chain," a "fool," a "frail . . . Creature," he writes "this little Piece" for God's "dear sake."[76]

Restored in later life, Wigglesworth preached intermittently; he was wont to speak of a span of twenty years of his life during which he was "almost buried alive."[77] Yet he lived to be seventy-four. Surveying Wigglesworth's entire career and personality, it is hard to escape the impression of a physical and nervous collapse, of which *The Day of Doom* was the dark flower. Thus the poem became the first in American literature of a number of "little pieces" derived from similar causes; we think, for example, of certain tales by Poe and Melville. At any rate, the "satanic kink," as a twentieth century poet might have called it, is the distinguishing fact in Wigglesworth's personality as contrasted with the even moral temper of Anne Bradstreet. This warp we must keep in mind to understand the excesses of the poem. Wigglesworth's ineradicable fear was that he might prefer even the highest satisfactions—his studies, his pupils' happiness, his peace of mind—to meditation upon God. Perhaps John L. Sibley's evaluation is still the best:

> Free from cant, conscientious even to morbidness, perpetually praying and struggling against pride and what he regarded as his besetting sins, aspiring after a religious state altogether unattainable, ever faithful to the extent of his strength and capacity, and fearful lest his interest in his pupils and others should steal away his heart from God, in whom his trust was so strong as to appear almost ridiculous to men who regard the Almighty as quite indifferent to their fortunes.[78]

Thus all other pleasures, all other purposes were secondary to this: always "to muse of the things of God."[79] Such introspection left its imprint on *The Day of Doom* in two ways. First, Wigglesworth described with Calvinistic zeal these apocalyptic moments; he was enchanted with the fiery splendor of the Judgment. Once accustomed to the ballad meter and the bumpy rhymes, the reader cannot help responding to this display of theological fireworks. The midnight "light," the "hideous cry of sinners," the abject flight from the "Presence," the Judge on his throne, the blast of the trump, the raising of the dead, the anguish and bliss alternating throughout the two hundred and twenty-four eight-line stanzas,—all such form a pageant which must stimulate, even if it is touched with absurdity, both believer and skeptic. This wild jamboree of light, darkness visible, din, and color must have been warming at the end of a drab Puritan day. Action is continuous and cosmic:

> And by and by the flaming Sky
> shall drop like molten Lead.[80]

One understands the remark made some fifty years after its publication that it would continue to be read until the moment of judgment itself. Few writings in America before 1800 throb more intensely with drama than Wigglesworth's *The Day of Doom*.

Secondly, in addition to the fierce intensity of Wigglesworth's musing on "the things of God," the poem reflects his own conscience, his imperious master throughout his life. When on the Sabbath a neighbor's barn-door swung to and fro in the wind, Wigglesworth suffered torments. What was his duty? Could he tell his friend and still show respect for the holy Sabbath? When his wife died, he said: "Oh it is a heart-cutting and astonishing stroke in itself."[81] Yet he added instantly: "Lord help me to bear it patiently and to profit by it."[82] From this same sensitivity derived the passionate desire in his poetry

> To set forth Truth, and win mens Souls to bliss.[83]

Besides the theatricals of his terrible Day, Wigglesworth sets forth also in the poem the arguments concerning man's destiny which he had debated in his own heart. Of his carefully reasoned conclusions the most famous is that which consigns the unbaptized infants to "the easiest room in Hell."[84] We return, in the end, after recognizing other qualities in the poem, to his impersonal, inexorable justice; we admire his subordination of all personal considerations to what he believed to be God's will.

Principles of poetry other than "edification" Wigglesworth, in theory at least, ignored. Thus he became an excellent example of the poet serving religion. He possessed, as we have seen, descriptive power, and so fervent was his emotion in contemplating the marvels of God that his graphic reporting of these bordered on poetry. No other Puritan poet realized better than Wigglesworth the ideal of "edification," and by his intensity he achieved something more: a breathless sense, less imaginatively conveyed in the prose of the Puritans, of the realities of bliss and torment which spurred them on. As we read Wigglesworth's "*Plain Meeter*" we understand what these concepts meant emotionally in their lives. What was Parnassus compared with Paradise?

> O glorious Place! where face to face
> Jehovah may be seen,

> By such as were sinners whilere
> and no dark vail between.
> Where the Sun shine, and light Divine,
> of Gods bright Countenance,
> Doth rest upon them every one,
> with sweetest influence.[85]

*   *   *

In contrast to that of Wigglesworth, the poetry of Edward Taylor is richer, more humane. Rigid theory dissolves in warmth and color; "edification," doctrine, learning, or ingenuities are vitalized by this poet's passionate nature. Although Taylor's verse was known to nineteenth century literary historians, the full revelation of his poetic powers belongs to our own time. As his important poems have come to light, their realism, their density, their melodic harshness, so to speak, have found affinities, in the judgment of scholars, not only in John Donne, in Richard Crashaw, and in other metaphysicals but in modern poetry. At this very moment Taylor's verse enjoys continual appreciation and revaluation. He is linked with the baroque tradition;[86] he is hailed, both in content and method, as an authentic metaphysical;[87] or he is flatly designated the most remarkable American poet prior to Philip Freneau.[88] Whatever his relative rank in the hierarchy of poets, he has, at least for the moment, eclipsed all other American Puritan versifiers. His writing is fascinating, but we must remember that in some ways Taylor is hardly more than a decade old; this is his day. Had Anne Bradstreet's best poetry remained unknown until 1939, she might have inspired a similar cult.[89]

We know something of Taylor's early life in the Colony and at Harvard, but little of the years of his lonely pastorate at Westfield, Massachusetts. Cotton Mather refers to his devoted presence at his frontier outpost as an "Angelical Conjunction."[90] For us the scanty biographical data are less enticing than the man himself "peeking," to use one of his favorite metaphors, from behind his verse. Samuel Sewall, his roommate in college, alludes to the power, and, we might infer, the intensity of one of his sermons, prepared "upon short warning"[91] at Old South Church. We see him, too, a little more clearly in the reminiscence of his grandson, Ezra Stiles: "A man of small stature but firm: of quick Passions—yet serious and grave."⁹² So it would seem: "quick Passions," and deep ones, too, whether we read the ecstatic "Hymn to Christ" or the short poem, "Upon the Sweeping Flood."⁹³ These two amazing stanzas of human love and divine response are unique in the poetry of seventeenth century America.

The body of Taylor's verse is substantial; filling a four hundred page manuscript volume, it includes elegies, lyrics, and, in particular, the two long groups of poems now referred to as "God's Determinations" and "Sacramental Meditations." The former, partly epical, partly lyrical, and often in dialogue suggestive of a morality play, reminds us repeatedly of Quarles, Herbert, and other seventeenth century English poets; "God's Determinations" relates the story of man's fall and his redemption through the doctrine of the New Covenant. The "Meditations," in number about two hundred, records the hopes and fears of the soul in its relations to the Creator. For his purpose the poet employs groups of from five to twelve six-line stanzas. Considered in its entirety, this verse of Taylor's wearies by its repetition, its extravagance of language, and by an innate tension not always pleasant. But we read on with increasing amazement at its sensuous qualities and at its brilliance of analogy and metaphor. For the specialist it continues to provide opportunities for analysis of the techniques of contrast, condensation, or paradox.⁹⁴

In all such poetic devices Taylor was an audacious experimenter. If it was sinful, as Wigglesworth appeared to believe, to woo the art of poetry for its own sake, then Taylor was indeed an offending soul. We cannot explain his deliberate roughness, his calculated marriage of the abstract and concrete, his love of the bizarre harmony of strange lines as solely inspired by "edification" or by a desire for ingenuities which would fix the individual in the paths of righteousness. What seventeenth century metaphysical poets were in his library we are not sure, but on some days in the lonely study at Westfield he was quickened not only by his yearning for God but by the creative moments of the artist. It is, for instance, impossible not to feel, in addition to the spiritual experience of the man of God, poetic fulfillment in the close-packed metaphors of the following six lines:

> Adorn me, Lord, with Holy Huswifry:
> All blanch my Robes with Clusters of thy Graces:

> Thus lead me to thy threashold: give mine Eye
>   A Peephole there to see bright glories Chases.
> Then take mee in: I'le pay, when I possess
>   Thy Throne, to thee the Rent in Happiness.[95]

We must not expect this pioneer parson to transcend his own era; he shared the air breathed by Anne Bradstreet and Michael Wigglesworth, but his richer, more poetic nature developed techniques, perhaps unconsciously, for their own purposes. Without dwelling upon the details of this craft, we may pause over two or three qualities of Taylor's poetry which may persuade the European student of the unique charm of this Puritan dreamer. The first of these is his tone of joy (not unlike that of the mystic, though Taylor is not, strictly speaking, a mystic). His images of the "Divil," of hell, and of himself as a sinful creature are black and violent, but actually he is less concerned than the other poets with what Emily Dickinson calls "the underside of God's divinity." The residual mood is joy in Christ. If the soul is "lumpish" or a "Crumb of Dust,"[96] it is, nevertheless, always about to enter the company of "Angells Bright" or of "sparkling Spirits," amid flowers and "Pillars" or "Wreaths" of perfume. The saints sing as they ride to glory in "Christs Coach."[97] In Taylor's poetry man's story has a happy ending; Christ is less the judge than the consoler. Man is redeemed by love:

> But thou, sweet Lord, hast with thy golden Key
> Unlock[t] the Doore, and made a golden day.

> Once at the Feast, I saw thee Pearle-like stand
>   'Tween Heaven and Earth, where Heavens Bright glory all
> In streams fell on thee, as a floodgate and,
>   Like Sun Beams through thee on the World to Fall.[98]

Passages quoted elsewhere have already illustrated another quality of Taylor's poetry: its opulent, ecstatic use of the senses. Everywhere the imagery is rich and varied: the feeling of clothes upon the body; the taste of bread or meat; the scent of flowers or perfume; the sound of pipes or the viol; and, of course, the sight of "brightsome colours." Over this poetry, though balanced by intellectual and doctrinal concepts and by a strong if erratic craftsmanship, hovers a golden light. Most of all, Taylor holds our respect by his metaphors of common, intimate (sometimes too intimate) objects and incidents of daily life. Adjacent to abstract and complicated thought occur the homeliest of analogies.

That of the humble, contrite man as God's "spinning wheel," with its proliferated metaphor, is now a well-known passage in American literature; and there are literally scores of others in Taylor's poetry: a "Bottle Ale"; "an anvill Sparke"; a tinder box; a bellows; a golden spade; a purse; a wagon; a rusted lock; a bowling alley; and, of course, everywhere flowers, clouds, and birds. By all these Taylor interprets in one way or another the relations of God and man; altogether they represent what one critic calls Taylor's "domesticating of the Infinite."[93] Thus the soul turning to Christ for succor against the attacks of sin likens its enemy to a cur. Christ in reply, in the next poem, takes up the metaphor:

> And if he run an inch too fur,
> I'le Check his Chain, and rate the Cur.
> My Chick, keep close to mee.[100]

* * *

For the European, beginning the study of American literature, this portrait of the Puritan poet will not be out of place in a gallery of other seventeenth century practicers of the craft. Limited in theory, and often too obedient to this theory in actual performance, he offers, nevertheless, especially to those acquainted with his English and Continental antecedents and contemporaries, intellectual pleasure of a high order. If he was not as musical as Apollo's lute, neither was he altogether harsh and crabbed. Concerning other Puritan authors, criticism is changing daily. Other names and freshly revealed poems enlarge and qualify the canon of this seventeenth century verse. Possibly there will be other discoveries to outshine that of the poems of Edward Taylor. Yet a more forceful revolt than his against mere "edification" is unlikely to have occurred; whatever the shift of emphasis upon individuals, the dominant temper will probably not be defined as essentially different from that represented in this chapter. Religion, after all, religion of a particular kind, circumscribed the Puritan poet of America; only within his narrow, stipulated empire did he fashion for himself and his people his strange but not wholly unlovely palace of poetry.

CHAPTER II

THE POET OF THE ENLIGHTENMENT

COTTON Mather's essay on style (mentioned in the first chapter) foretells implicitly the doom of the Puritan poet. The craving for unholy forms of poetry, which Mather deplores, was to mean eventually a release from "edification" and from other somber trappings of the muse. This preface to the *Manuductio ad Ministerium* appeared in 1726. More than a century had passed since the founding of Plymouth Colony; obviously the subordination of poetry to theology could not escape the general challenge to Puritan thought and Puritan ways of life. In the following year Mather's kinsman, that sophisticated divine, Mather Byles, then twenty years old, published poems on the death of King George I and the accession of George II.

Byles was just beginning his career as preacher, loyalist, convivial dinner-guest, and punster. Confined to his house by the patriots, he delighted Boston by dispatching his sentinel on an errand and mounting guard over himself, declaring that he had been "guarded, reguarded, and disregarded."[1] Byles was a disciple of Dryden; and he corresponded with Pope. Much of his poetry was devotional, but much of it was not; and in his relish for gay verse we have hints of a new world of poetic theory now imminent. Indeed, it had arrived when a divine could write as follows to a lady who had asked him for the loan of his copy of the all-ruling poet:

> Go, my dear Pope, transport th'attentive fair,
> And soothe, with winning harmony, her ear.
> 'Twill add new graces to thy heav'nly song,
> To be repeated by her gentle tongue.[2]

For as the men and women of the eighteenth century looked on the smiling countryside and dreamed their dreams for the future of America, the reality of the Calvinistic nightmare faded. So faded, also, in both England and America, during the last years of the seventeenth century, the preoccupation with the supernatural, in life and in poetry. The influences of Locke and Hobbes included literature, and Richard Hurd remarked that the imagination would be forced "to ally herself with strict truth, if she would gain admittance into reasonable company."³ Those impulses in the art of poetry toward the secular, repressed by Anne Bradstreet and Edward Taylor, now reached in the mid-eighteenth century in America a conspicuous fulfillment. Although against poetry other enemies were to rise up, enemies almost as powerful as the bigotry of the seventeenth century; although the great leader of the age, Benjamin Franklin, thanked God that he had escaped "being a poet, most probably a very bad one,"⁴ still the poet of 1750 was a happier being than the poet of 1650, or at least a more rational one. In Byles's heroic couplets or in William Livingston's seven hundred lines, *Philosophic Solitude* (1747), we sense a different poetic temper. We are now to meet "The Poet of the Enlightenment."

He was to be better than the Poet of Puritanism,—better, and worse. Although after 1750 a few of the metaphysicals lingered on, as stubborn in the old forms as had been Jonathan Edwards in his championing of a dying Puritanism, most of the new poets had dismissed forever "edification," the anagram, the gnarled metaphor, and, above all, the extreme emotional experience,—ecstasy or penitence. Instead our first, casual glance detects a secular life, a schematic nature, lucid classical illustration, a somewhat stereotyped phraseology, "elegant numbers," and, it must be confessed, a refreshing order and clarity. Obviously the new poetry aimed, in the words of Hobbes, at "*steddy direction* to some approved end."⁵

At first the changes are startling: satire becomes at once a more brutal and a more finished weapon; religious vérse is more serene,— and more empty; and a thousand subjects inherent in the actual life of the colonies, from merino sheep to hasty-pudding, clutter this correct, facile verse. Poetry has become unashamedly imitative; no longer are literary debts, as in the case of Edward Taylor, conjectural. Denham, Milton, Dryden, Pope, Churchill, Swift, and Goldsmith have crossed the Atlantic. Altogether poetry now offers an exciting pageant of man in America. Within half a century it is so utterly altered in content from that of the poetry of Wigglesworth

38

or of Anne Bradstreet that we are eager to know the causes of this revolution in art.

* * *

With these causes most of us are at least vaguely familiar. After 1687, the date of the *Principia*, the universe, including even this tiny corner of the world, this New England, had become more and more Newtonian. This cosmos, aggressively mathematical, fulfilling itself in inexorable law, whether in the interstellar spaces or in the pollen of a flower, did not at once expel supernaturalism. A storm might still mean God's displeasure. Yet inevitably the descendants of the first Puritans, who had themselves been fascinated by their own limited science,[6] were, in the second and third decades of the eighteenth century, tempted and sometimes converted by the religious and social corollaries of this new absolute. Isaac Greenwood, for example, and John Winthrop, Professor of "natural philosophy" at Harvard[7] during approximately the four decades prior to the Revolution, intimated that the meaning of life might be found less in the doctrine of God's grace and in the correlated dogmas than in man's reason. For the stupendous character of Newton's achievement seemed in itself a proof of the almost limitless power of this faculty of man. Thus Philip Freneau sang:

> Great Frame! what wonders we survey,
> In part alone, from day to day!
> And hence the reasoning, human soul
> Infers an author of the whole.[8]

In fact, for the Puritan there was something insidious in Newton's frank invitation to give free rein to human reason since, after all, this had played within the framework of Calvinism so important a part in the theological drama. If we study the functioning of the human intellect in the writings of, say, John Wise, who considered man a reasoning animal, or in those of Roger Williams, who so highly esteemed man's understanding, or of Jonathan Mayhew, who urged his followers to shape their own destinies,[9] one conclusion is inescapable: some of these seventeenth century ways of thought were a prelude to the Newtonian symphony of God and man. Indeed, Petrus Ramus, the qualifier of Calvinistic doctrines, had aroused the hope that with patient effort man could begin to comprehend the universe.

Thus this "fifth column" had already cleared the way for the Newtonian invasion. More and more man marvelled at the symmetry of these laws, and more and more he applied them directly to his mundane affairs, studying botany, astronomy, and, as much as possible, chemistry or geology. The eighteenth century individual read his almanacs and practiced his commerce in this brave Newtonian world,[10] which had challenged the undemonstrable thesis that man was depraved. As a matter of fact, in this universe, the contrary seemed more credible. Was he not good? As he looked around at the peaceful villages and fields or up at the "spangled heavens," he might well think, in contrast to the earlier century's somewhat pessimistic conclusions, that

In Reason's ear they all rejoice.[11]

But reason could not, did not wish to prove that God had fully revealed himself; it stopped abruptly before the miraculous. What could reason offer man as a working religion? From the very nature of things it predicated an "Author" of the universe, a creator. The great Watchmaker had wrought this vast and delicate machine; then left it to tick by its own laws. The Landlord had built the house, but had withdrawn. God was, indeed, a dim being compared with the meddlesome God of the Calvinist. To Cotton Mather's recurrent question, "What can I see of the glorious God in this occurrence?" the new religion gave no response. Nature did not bow to man's particular needs; Freneau's lines expressed this truth well:

> Could she descend from that great plan
> To work unusual things for man,
> To suit the insect of an hour—·
> This would betray a want of power.[12]

Lord Herbert of Cherbury or Lord Shaftsbury or that practical printer, inventor, business-man, and statesman of our own country, Benjamin Franklin, agreed, with differing degrees of emphasis, not on "grace" or a "New Covenant," but on a universe of law comprehensible to man's reason.

Such thinkers were, of course, deists, rejecting the traditional in religion, the supernatural, the fantastic fables of priests. They envisioned a new millennium, in which man, turning his back on these ancient specters, might apply celestial laws to his economics, his education, his society, his personal life, and might strive to create a Heavenly City on earth.[13] Such was the religion of the Enlightenment, which though damned by its enemies as "infidelity," swiftly pervaded the thought of the age:

> Do we want [said Thomas Paine] to contemplate his power? We see it in the immensity of the creation. Do we want to contemplate his wisdom? We see it in the unchangeable order by which the incomprehensible Whole is governed. Do we want to contemplate his munificence? We see it in the abundance with which he fills the earth. Do we want to contemplate his mercy? We see it in his not withholding that abundance even from the unthankful. In fine, do we want to know what God is? Search not the book called the scripture, which any human hand might make, but the scripture called the Creation.[14]

From the harmonious correlation of these concepts of the scientist and of the deist there developed under the Enlightenment other ideas which these architectonic thinkers derived from the "great Original." Never has the universe been more tidily explained. In fact, a nineteenth century thinker was to inveigh against this precision as "spiritual paralysis": "I say," growled Thomas Carlyle, "nothing left but a Mechanical life. . . . Mechanism in the Universe has in the fatalest way missed the secret of the Universe altogether."[15] Perhaps. We may look backward to the Poet of Puritanism with his miracles or forward to the Poet of Romanticism with his exaltations and frustrations, but there is a coolly satisfying temper in this deistic matrix for poetry. For these new concepts were born of the central conviction that God was an impersonal architect whose creations, including man himself, were animated by scientific law. Reading Newton, Locke, Tindal or other rationalists, the eighteenth century poet might well be hospitable to the patterns of environmentalism, "the great-chain-of-being," the natural rights philosophy, progress, humanitarianism, and science itself.[16]

*   *   *

Such creeds linked themselves immediately with the theory and practice of poetry in eighteenth century America. At every turn we feel the importance of science and reason, in subject and in method. In Mrs. Centlivre's play, *The Basset Table*, the English heroine, fascinated by botany, exclaims when her lover urges her to flee with him: "What! and leave my microscope?"[17] Indeed, we are wrong if we think that poetry will wither and die under the glare of Newton's astral mechanics. On the contrary, now is ushered in one of the great ages of English poetry.

And across the Atlantic spread the new gospel! All these ideas of the Enlightenment find a not ignoble, though hardly inspired, place in American verse, even in the songs of agriculture written by the "Connecticut Wits."[18] In his pastoral poem, *Greenfield Hill*, Timothy Dwight celebrates the "happy few" in America who enjoy this blessed land's "sweet competence."[19] In similar fashion all the reasoned conclusions of the eighteenth century social thinkers find expression in Joel Barlow's *Columbiad*:

> Equality of Right [he sings] is nature's plan;
> And following nature is the march of man.[20]

How delightfully characteristic of this pattern for poetry is Barlow's tribute to Thomas Godfrey, glazier, mathematician, and inventor of the quadrant:

> To guide the sailor in his wandering way,
> See Godfrey's glass reverse the beams of day.
> His lifted quadrant to the eye displays
> From adverse skies the counteracting rays;
> And marks, as devious sails bewilder'd roll,
> Each nice gradation from the stedfast pole.[21]

We look ahead, in contrast, to the wild, romantic Ahab, in Melville's *Moby-Dick*, renouncing science: "Foolish toy! .... Curse thee, thou quadrant!"[22]

In such a world of ideas the eighteenth century American poet lived, a world as different from that of Michael Wigglesworth as broad daylight is from dusk. Here were bred, quite naturally, the new American's philosophies of poetry, conscious or unconscious. What were they? No detailed study of theories concerning the many varied forms, like the pastoral or the mock-epic, exists for English poetry of the century,[23] and American poetry lacks even partial studies of the problem, such as we find in analyses, for example, of Alexander Pope.[24] We must, once again, make our own synthesis, and the principles adduced will be general in character. The distinctions which exist between Timothy Dwight's and Joel Barlow's theories of the epic, if such can be formulated, will be reserved for another occasion though we shall note common underlying conceptions in these poets. These opinions must be deduced, for the most part, from specific lines in the poetry of the "Wits" or of the Philadelphia Group, from their criticism of books, from their letters, or even from their footnotes, as in those attached to Trumbull's *M'Fingal*. Prefaces or definitions of poetic aims hardly occur in American literature before Bryant and Longfellow; and subversive theories indigenously American begin with Whitman. Of the leading American poets of the eighteenth century only John Trumbull, chiefly through his critical papers, offers the semblance of carefully reasoned principles.[25]

In making such a synthesis we shall at once be impressed by American dependence, even more docile than that of the seventeenth century, upon European and particularly upon English models. The earlier poet had shown a species of originality; he was, perhaps, not unaided by his very isolation from his English cousins. In the seventeenth century bookstores hardly existed; libraries were small. His loneliness may have helped Edward Taylor to carve out metaphysical patterns of his own; the lack of communication with Europe had its hard-won advantages. In the eighteenth century, however, the colonial intimacy with English poetry amounted to sycophancy. Byles's friendship with Pope and Freneau's profusely annotated copy of the *Essay on Man* tell a plain story of uncritical admiration. Libraries and bookstores were flooded with the poetry and philosophy of the Age of Reason.[26]

Indeed, at times this American poetry was directly in debt to European prose statements of theory. The recently-defined obligation of the "Connecticut Wits" to *Elements of Criticism* by the Scottish thinker, Lord Kames, probably represents a *type* of such influence.[27] We need very much to know how widely read in America were the prefaces of Dryden; or how much Pope's particular utterances on poetry were studied.[28] Yet, lacking at present this knowledge, we incline to think the dependence sprang from the poetry itself, from tacit acceptance of the attitudes of great English poets. In any case, whatever the precise sources, the imitation was copious, universal, and sometimes sedulous.

We shall find, then, American theories of poetry in debt, as it were, not to any one corner of English literary life, as in the seventeenth century (for example, to Quarles or Donne), but in broad outline to English poetry from John Milton to William Cowper. Moreover, the protests against ancient idols were reënacted on a small scale; in this native verse were echoes of Johnson's repudiation of the metaphysicals, of the distrust of "inspiration," of the preference for the general over the particular.[29] Into the somewhat crude American temple moved the triple-headed god: Authority, Reason, and Taste.[30]

Yet, though always thoroughly conditioned by English attitudes and though never deeply original, the theories, as well as the practice, were colored by the American experience. Thus Timothy Dwight inflated (almost to the point of collapse) English pastoral theories to include certain primitive American materials, and although Trumbull's satire, *M'Fingal*, reminds us of Butler and Churchill, it has a native quality. Trumbull, indeed, in his youthful *Essay on the Uses and Advantages of the Fine Arts* (1770), attacked the affectations of English literature and protested against its worn-out poetic diction.[31] In particular, he amplified for his own purposes two types of burlesque, high and low, and laid down laws on metrics, imagery, and language.[32] Likewise, the poetry of Philip Freneau, though never unconscious of its British masters, shows us a nature never found in Pope's *Windsor Forest*, namely, the trees, flowers, and birds of New Jersey!—and of the West Indies. Hence there occurred a broadening, perhaps a cheapening, of the English theories.

The first English directive for this American verse of the eighteenth century involved form; poetry was no longer to be in the baroque tradition, but in the neoclassic. Newton in science; Shaftesbury in religion; Waller, Dryden, and Pope in poetry! In their techniques these American poets accepted Dryden and "the syllable-counting" Pope, with his logic, his meticulous line, his elegance. Francis Knapp's epistle to him, amusing now, symbolized a vogue which endured well into the nineteenth century:

> Hail, sacred Bard! a Muse unknown before
> Salutes thee from the bleak *Atlantic* shore.
> To our dark world thy shining page is shown,
> And *Windsor's* gay retreat becomes our own.
> . . . .
> Where-e'er we dip in thy delightful page,
> What pompous scenes our busy thoughts engage![33]

Such couplets became the most frequently used of all verse forms by our eighteenth century poets.[34] These they studied not only in Pope, but in Waller, Dryden, and others, and, like English readers, they delighted in the arid (so it seems today) *Art of English Poetry* (1702), by Edward Bysshe.[35] From such poets and critics they borrowed, too, the neoclassic apparatus: the gods and goddesses; the cold-hearted Greek and Latin fables; the classical allusions; the shallow personifications. Wistfully our countrified poets emulated the refinement, the conversational ease, and also the exclusion of certain subjects, emotions, and language as unfit for gentlemanly verse. Their allegiance was, among kindred deities, to "godlike Addison," to "thrice happy Dryden," and to "heav'nly Pope."[36]

American poets of the eighteenth century used, then, the neoclassic forms of English verse: heroic couplets, octosyllabics (so dear to the "Connecticut Wits" and Freneau), the Spenserian stanza, and also, of course, various types of blank verse, similar to Milton's, Cowper's, or Thomson's. Even when our tyros shared the stir of emotion heralding the advent of romantic poetry, the old rules of poetry still prevailed, although there were some mild violations in practice, as in the lyrics of Freneau.[37] Thomas Odiorne, an obscure poet of the latter years of the century, has lately been revived as a forerunner of Wordsworth,[38] and we shall meet with other deviations in practice. Nevertheless, in the main, neoclassic principles held undisputed sway. John Adams's hope, voiced in a letter to John Trumbull on April 28, 1785, represented a general poetic ambition of the epoch: "to see our young America in Possession of an Heroick Poem, equal to those the most esteemed in any Country."[39] As already mentioned, the research which will determine the precise influence of Pope is still to be done, but even after the popularity of Thomson's *Seasons*, the first American edition of which appeared in 1777,[40] one may guess that the former's supremacy was unshaken.

Since explicit definitions of poetic aims are few, we may pause over some observations by John Trumbull, the least inarticulate in such matters of all the "Connecticut Wits." His biographer remarks: "There is no question that he accepted Johnson's dictum that 'the business of a poet is to examine, not the individual, but the species; to remark general properties and large appearances.'"[41]

The basic rules of the game Trumbull evidently regarded, like his fellow-poets, as really settled forever. The line ran straight from Aristotle, through Horace, Boileau, and Dryden, to Pope. Mankind could hope for nothing better in poetry; and improvement could only come from effort *within* the rules. To be sure, as a boy Trumbull formed for himself special, subsidiary mandates concerning description, selection, arrangement, and similar poetic problems.[42] Nevertheless, nothing exceptional, either in feeling or expression, could be expected; moreover, it was not desired.

Thus Trumbull's ideas concerning the mock-epic, a form in which he became an expert, were essentially derivative although modified by the peculiar demands of his American subject. Since Timothy Dwight, too, seemed to follow, if vaguely, the principles of Aristotle, Trumbull included him in his list of the major epic writers, above Lucan and not far below Ariosto![43] Without apology Trumbull imitated the great English satirists, and his tribute to Pope would have been endorsed, presumably, by every poet mentioned in this chapter:

> Pope [he declared] in his manner of writing is an inimitable Original. . . . By manner of writing I mean method, style, expression, versification &c. As to his versification I do not regard the objection, that it is formed upon Dryden's. I do not call him an Imitator, who improves an Art to a perfection of which his Master had no Idea.[44]

What was the eighteenth century poet to sing in his fluent blank verse, in his heroic couplets or his octosyllabics? Religion? Yes, but only as one phase of man's multiple life. As reason had banished the tortuous anagram from the language of poetry, so it had exiled the priests' preposterous themes of grace, election, or the New Covenant. Poetry was now to be not the handmaiden of religion, but the servant (a practical word for a practical usage) of man. Its basic aim was to mirror in perspective the manifold activities of reasoning humanity. To adapt Pope's famous saying: the proper study of the poet was mankind. Reason, nature, progress, humanitarianism,—the poet was to give his readers repeated expositions of these spacious ideas. Man himself was but a tiny fraction in the mathematics of this gigantic universe, but he should be informed about the relations of its laws to his mind. Poetry was to be functional; to reveal man to himself in all his relationships.[45]

In both England and America man's kinship to nature was discussed endlessly in this equable verse, whether in Thomson's *Seasons*, so popular in America, or in Timothy Dwight's *Greenfield Hill*. Although belonging to another age, the chapter called "Commodity" in Emerson's *Nature* (1836) seems to be in debt to this ceaseless poetic preoccupation with the usefulness of nature.[46] Thus both English and American poems delight in gardening, botany, agriculture, and in the phenomena and beneficent laws of nature. Thomson's poems on the mist and the rainbow include, respectively, discussions of evaporation and the prism;[47] and with a similar delight in utility, Dwight describes how

> . . . . Rivers, with foamy course,
> Pour o'er the ragged cliff the white cascade,
> And roll unnumber'd mills.[48]

On a different level the eighteenth century poet's contemplation of the natural world postulates a God at once nobler and more credible, he believed, than the irascible deity depicted in seventeenth century verse. As a modern critic says, "The old God of Judea was in these men's minds not great enough for this wonderful world. He was convicted on two counts, for playing favourites and for breaking the rules!"[49] This vision of a limitless universe moving in a divine harmony of natural law stirred the American poet, too, to moods not unlike those of Addison's hymn or of Pope's *Essay on Man*:

> All are but parts of one stupendous whole,
> Whose body Nature is, and God the Soul.[50]

As eighteenth century poetic theory in America linked man with the "stupendous whole," so it encouraged a kind of forum with argument concerning his religious and social beliefs. In "The Power of Fancy" Freneau echoes the ideas of the deists; in *The Triumph of Infidelity* Dwight denounces their godless creed. Or in *The Columbiad* Joel Barlow ponders on liberty, equality, and humanitarianism. As, more and more, verse became a useful weapon in politics and war, the techniques of the English satirists were emulated, though in practice, for example, in Freneau's *The Rising Glory of America* or *The British Prison-Ship*, American satire sank at times into invective hardly better than a journalist's lampoon. Indeed, we detect a corruption of the aims of the English masters; poetry on the utility of nature can hardly be more pedestrian than David Humphreys's matter-of-fact verses on the loom and wool:

> Then, rous'd from lethargies—up! men! increase,
> In every vale, on every hill, the fleece![51]

Thus in America the English criteria reappear, including the theory that verse should depict man in polite society: cultivated man becomes a symbol of the refinement of the race.[52] The levels are various and the subjects diverse, but the target of the American poets, too, was always man in his environment, especially in the environment of this new country.

It may be argued that from this environment the American poets added something to their own poetic theories, however unexpressed in preface or manifesto. Surely no eighteenth century background for the creation of poetry was more unusual than these colonies fringing the Atlantic seaboard and the wilderness. As Timothy Dwight gazed down from his hilltop home upon the Connecticut countryside, his blank verse was conventional, but his dreams were boundless:

> . . . . Hail, O hail
> My much-lov'd native land! New Albion hail![53]

A passion for long passages on this pastoral America obsessed these poets, as well as a curiosity concerning its hidden future. So numerous are these speculations about the *American* man's destiny, that the familiar Augustan patterns seem mildly altered. If the conviction that the major theme of verse should be America is not in itself precisely a new poetic theory, it is at any rate the beginning of a theory. This is the embryo of the "American Myth," the idealized America which was to become conscious theory for Walt Whitman and Hart Crane.[54] This belief in the importance of America as a subject for poetry affected every eighteenth century poet.

* * *

In practice, all these theories, including even this dream of America, appear, in our eighteenth century poetry, utilitarian. Demanding little craftsmanship or high imagination, they encouraged mediocrity. A few political ideas, a talent for exposition, deft octo-syllabics,—and lo! here was a poem! Indeed, it is a long and tedious journey through these American deserts of blank verse and heroic couplets written before 1800. For in performance this literal verse seems almost to parody the principles it follows so closely, and to add a new boredom through its insistence on America's own history and growth. In satire, the acute elegance of Dryden becomes the vulgarity of Jonathan Odell, who thus addresses Washington:

> Go, wretched author of thy country's grief,
> Patron of villainy, of villains chief.[55]

The public taste was low and unformed, as in England, but, in addition, the cultivated readers were fewer, and often the principles originating in the forceful minds of Dryden and Pope were drained of their vitality. We look in vain for an *Absalom and Achitophel* or a *Rape of the Lock*.

Sometimes, however, even in this illiterate, confused America of the Revolutionary era, the expressions of these poetic theories, particularly in their emphasis upon man's place in the "stupendous whole," attains dignity. The mosaic of eighteenth century concepts (Newton, Locke, Hobbes, Pope) appears with a species of corporate worth in the verse of two groups, namely in those of Philadelphia and Connecticut, and with grace in one poet who excelled them all, both in his practice of current theories and in his adaptation of these to the American life about him. The serious poetry of Philip Freneau, alone among these American poets, is relatively free from the absurd and the trivial; among eighteenth century poets he is still unforgotten. Remembered in national history as "that rascal Freneau"[56] (Washington's rueful tribute to his satire), he retains a place in our literary history for a few memorable lyrics. In fact, the study of our civilized verse might well begin with Freneau; it is fair to repeat the platitude that he is the "Father of American Poetry." More will be said later concerning his achievement.

The existence of two or more circles of poets is suggestive. Oddly enough, the theory and practice of poetry in eighteenth century America drew writers into coteries more definite than those of the first half of the nineteenth. In such groupings political influences were powerful. In their youth the "Connecticut Wits" were sound Federalists, and common ideas drew together the Princetonians, Freneau, Brackenridge, and Madison.[57] We must study the actual performance of these poets, but for a moment we should pause over lesser figures who reflected the current temper in poetry.

Thus the influence of Dryden in America is neatly illustrated in the writing of that civilized minister, Benjamin Colman, particularly in *Elijah's Translation* (1707); and the influence of Pope in the poem of Mather Byles's, already mentioned, "To *********
Desiring to Borrow Pope's Homer." Both these clergymen lived stormy lives, and there is something ironical, even pathetic in their devotion to a classic calm which they seldom experienced. In *Philosophic Solitude*, William Livingston, at the time of its publication twenty-four years old and destined to a life of action, swears that he will remain among his books: Virgil, Milton, Pope, Dryden, Watts, Locke, Raleigh, Denham. In his library he will

> ... live retir'd, contented, and serene,
> Forgot, unknown, unenvied, and unseen.[58]

Livingston was not insincere; he was merely an American disciple of the poetic theories of his time.

Livingston lived long enough to see challenged the ideals for poetry which he had outlined so prettily in his *Philosophic Solitude*. In the last quarter of the century mild protests arose against the standard classical patterns from poets who were afflicted with pre-romantic moods, especially from those who were speculative concerning man's relation to nature. Somewhat belated in America, this growing discontent paralleled that in England, where Gray, Thomson, and Collins had raised fresh banners.[59] This uneasiness was less a revolt against the official poetic creed than a qualification. The softer note in poetry was less discernible among the "Connecticut Wits," so impeccably conservative, than in Provost Smith's group at the "College of Philadelphia," in which Francis Hopkinson, partly because of his eminence as a musical composer, was eventually to become the most conspicuous poet. More literary than the little band at Princeton, whose leader was Freneau, more flexible in mind than the "Wits," this group became a nursery for a civilized tradition in American poetry. These were men and women of refinement speaking reasonably and elegantly to each other and, in a more remote way, to the outside citizenry.[60]

*   *   *

Thus Philadelphia was the cradle of more than American liberty. Besides Franklin and other statesmen, here had lived Elizabeth Graeme Ferguson,[61] her friend, the poet, Nathaniel Evans, and our first dramatist, Thomas Godfrey,—also a poet. Here, for these gifted writers the benevolent William Smith, Provost of the University of Pennsylvania, provided a magazine. Here were discussed the Latin classics, belles-lettres, and the music and painting in which some of these authors were skillful amateurs. Here, too, the eighteenth century regulations concerning poetry were treated more light-heartedly than by the "Connecticut Wits," who showed a tendency to dress the Muse in tie-wig and breeches. Mrs. Ferguson must have been excellent company. Addressing Nathaniel Evans, she parodies lines in "Eloisa to Abelard":

> How happy is the country Parson's lot?
> Forgetting *Bishops*, as by *them* forgot.[62]

Until the end of the century this cultivated circle was to implement, always gracefully, the theories of the age, and not without a critical spirit. The orthodox poets of Connecticut would not have been altogether happy in Philadelphia.

It is tempting to linger over this cheerful little group of poets, not unlike in spirit the clientele of young Irving in New York some fifty years later. Mrs. Ferguson, Evans (and presently the accomplished William Cliffton), and Thomas Godfrey caught from the Latin classics a Horatian temper hopelessly beyond the reach of the heavy-footed "Wits." Their delight in Thomson and Collins, as well as in Churchill, their incorrigible good-humor, their agile light verse made Philadelphia the sole center in America for the literary amenities of the Enlightenment. Their poetry, though often, as in the case of Hopkinson, sharpened by anger, showed on the whole a serenity of mind which, in contrast to what was written before and after, has become a welcome enrichment of our literary history. We are right in suspecting that with this spirit that amiable citizen of the world, Benjamin Franklin, was not unconnected; he had, indeed, high hopes for the culture of this community (without, of course, particular interest in its poetry). One of Evans's most diverting poems is addressed to this philosopher after the poet had heard him play enchantingly upon the harmonica.[63]

Without praising too highly the gay lyrics of Mrs. Ferguson or the easy Latin verse of Evans, we may admire the urbane relationships of these poets in this provincial America, so far from the London of which they often talked. In March, 1732, for example, Thomas Godfrey waited upon James Blair Logan, "a gentleman of universal learning and the best judge of books in these parts."[64] The particular books under discussion were for the "Library Company of Philadelphia," and so for everyone's use. Over this coterie hovers an aura of cultural philanthropy. Evans published a correspondence between himself and "Laura" (Mrs. Ferguson), and addressed his imitation of Horace to Godfrey. After Evans's unfortunate death at the age of twenty-five, Dr. Smith acknowledged Mrs. Ferguson's aid in the publication of the young poet's works. And so on. No verse of the first or even of the second order ever came from this group; one must not expect too much. Yet here was a miniature Augustan circle in America, an exciting fulfillment of certain poetic theories of the age.

Thomas Godfrey predeceased his devoted friend, Evans, by four years; the united spans of these two poets hardly exceed half a century. Something more than friendship inspired Evans's admiration of Godfrey, and called forth his best poetry, including his "Elegy" (1772), on the death of Godfrey. Evans recognized the now obvious fact that Godfrey was the most versatile writer of the Philadelphia Group. Son of the mathematician of the same name,[65] the younger Thomas Godfrey early left the watchmaker, to whom he had been apprenticed, to play with subtler time-schemes in verse and the drama. This opportunity Godfrey owed to Provost Smith, who though no poet himself was often the stimulator of poetry in other men. Through Smith, too, Godfrey became in 1758 an ensign and served in the march against Fort Duquesne. At Wilmington, North Carolina, where he lived for several years, he was hard at work on his tragedy, *The Prince of Parthia*, when suddenly he died, too soon to know that this was to be the first drama in blank verse performed upon the American stage. His other legacy to American poetry was the posthumous collection of his works (1765), with its preface by Evans, who refers to it as "the first of the kind that this Province has produced."[66]

In the five hundred line poem in this collection called "The Court of Fancy," Godfrey acknowledged his obligation to Pope; his "Dithyrambic on Wine" (a liquid he never drank) and his other songs, odes, or elegies mirror the usual English models.[67] He had mastered the orthodox poetic language; and some passages indicate that he responded to the transitional influences which so mitigated the conventionality of Freneau. Even in his pathetically short career, both in *The Prince of Parthia* and in his other verse, Godfrey recorded concepts broader than those which molded the "Connecticut Wits." He was almost as much Elizabethan as Augustan, and though various voices are audible in his tragedy, we hear most clearly those of Shakespeare and Nicholas Rowe.[68] "The Court of Fancy" he had modeled upon "The House of Fame" of Chaucer, to whom he gives thanks and in whose spirit he composed also a version of "The Parliament of Fowls." Something about Godfrey, despite his naïveté, captures our regard today, something more than the tragedy of his premature death and his triumph in creating the first American play; his was an amiable and rich nature denied full development. He himself sings:

> How sweet the eloquence of dying men!
> Hence Poets feign'd the music of the Swan,
> When death upon her lays his icy hand,
> She melts away in melancholy strains.[69]

The Philadelphia Circle comes to life still more vigorously in Godfrey's friend and fellow-dramatist, the composer, allegorist, and wit, Francis Hopkinson. Like Godfrey, Hopkinson was at home in neoclassic principles. He was receptive to the eighteenth century concepts of poetry, agreeing that it should describe man and all his various ways of life; but he loved to embroider these formalities, sometimes with serious purpose, more often with a whimsical fancy. Again we sense something different in this Southern air, for Hopkinson, though as briar-like in mind as Trumbull, was gentler in his satire than any of the "Connecticut Wits."

We see Hopkinson today pretty clearly, through his portrait and through the reminiscences of others. He was a civilized American Augustan, with embellishments of his own, both for his way of living and for his verse. John Adams's somewhat puzzled but vivid letter to his wife still offers the best vignette of the lively Hopkinson. I went, wrote Adams,

> to see Mr. Peale's painter's room. . . . At this shop I met Mr. Francis Hopkinson, late a Mandamus Counsellor of New Jersey, now a member of the Continental Congress, who, it seems, is a native of Philadelphia, a son of a prothonotary of this county, who was a person much respected. The son was liberally educated, and is a painter and a poet. I have a curiosity to penetrate a little deeper into the bosom of this curious gentleman, and may possibly give you some more particulars concerning him. He is one of your pretty, little, curious, ingenious men. His head is not bigger than a large apple. . . . I have not met with anything in natural history more amusing and entertaining than his personal appearance; yet he is genteel and well bred, and is very social.[70]

"Curious" he was, indeed! *The Miscellaneous Essays and Occasional Writings of Francis Hopkinson, Esq.* (1792) approve John Adams's adjective, "ingenious." Some of his verse, such as the hilarious satire, "The New Roof," deserves reprinting as much as his famous jingle, *The Battle of the Kegs* (1778). These twenty-two four-line stanzas, with their astonishing resemblance, as "fourteeners," to the rhythms of Wigglesworth's *Day of Doom*, differ from the ordinary neoclassic verse (in which Hopkinson was also accomplished); they are in the ballad or broadside tradition, which produced so many songs of the Revolution:

> Gallants attend and hear a friend,
> Trill forth harmonious ditty,
> Strange things I'll tell which late befel
> In Philadelphia city.[71]

The "strange things" deepened into the din of artillery:

> The cannons roar from shore to shore,
> The small arms make a rattle;
> Since wars began I'm sure no man
> E'er saw so strange a battle.[72]

To this day many an American schoolboy knows the story: how powder-kegs, set afloat as a kind of guided missile, floated down the river to terrify the British invaders. *The Battle of the Kegs* is a robust and hearty song. What interests us is the creation, as an offspring of the eighteenth century tradition, of this salty, humorous ballad within the elegant Philadelphia Circle. It has no rival among the productions of the "Connecticut Wits" except, perhaps, in Lemuel Hopkins's burlesque verses. To Philadelphia we must turn again for the freer impulses of American eighteenth century poetry.

*　　*　　*

As a matter of fact, the easy-going interpretation by the Philadelphia Group of the poetic theories of the Enlightenment was less characteristic of the century's literary history than the orthodoxy of the "Connecticut Wits," whose prominence as men of affairs enhanced their fame as poets. Such confusion of business and literature was long to be a familiar story in American letters. Despite differences in ages, occupations, and personalities, these able men were a closely-knit fraternity representing Federalist politics, Calvinistic religion, and Augustan literary traditions. Save for Joel Barlow's later Jacobinism, few heresies of any kind, least of all literary, dimmed their shining, united faith in the established order. We may, as we read on in the period, prefer the whimsical rhymes of Francis Hopkinson, but this huge monolith of verse built of heroic couplets and octosyllabics by six or seven poets is impressive, even if humorously so. Merely the labor consumed in Joel Barlow's titanic *Columbiad* commands respect. Ridiculous as an epic, it suggests the massive ambitions of the "Wits," not only for the theme of America, but for creating poetry in the only true faith of Milton, Dryden, and Pope.

Living their full lives in the Revolutionary and post-Revolutionary years, the "Wits" seem almost as anachronistic in their literary principles, as in those of religion and government.[73] We have observed in the Philadelphians an awareness of the pre-romantic mood, and we shall see the influence of this upon the lyrics of Freneau. No romantic weakness, however, delays the march of reason—a favorite word among the "Wits"—in the far-flung couplets of these coöperative poets; throughout their lives they imitated without embarrassment or fatigue their English contemporaries. *The Progress of Dulness*, Trumbull's youthful college poem, betrays its debts not merely to Butler, Swift, and Churchill, but specifically to *The Dunciad*.[74] Likewise, Timothy Dwight's *Conquest of Canäan*, which he announced as the first epic written in America,[75] and which needs (so said Trumbull) a lightning rod[76] for its innumerable thunderstorms, was a startling blend of *Paradise Lost* and Fenelon's *The Adventures of Telemachus*. Other debts envelop this imitative poetry, such as Dwight's (in *Greenfield Hill*) to Denham and Goldsmith or that of David Humphreys to Pope, until the individual traits of these American poets seem lost in the Englishmen they emulate.

Indeed, so ill-digested was this mass of English poetry, that we may question the "Wits'" actual comprehension of what they had swallowed. It is, for example, unlikely that Dwight and Humphreys sensed, as did Trumbull, the very real difference between the metrical patterns of Dryden and Pope. An excess of literary taste they assuredly lacked; these octosyllabics and heroic couplets became almost a formula, a style of writing inherent in the usage of the day rather than in any understanding of the varying techniques of the English poets. This fault is less demonstrable in Trumbull, who studied both Butler and Churchill; he realized fully the peculiar sharpness of the latter. Yet the hodge-podge of influences in the verse of Dwight and Humphreys warns us not to think of the "Wits" as really men of letters; they were national figures using the weapon of verse for the practical purposes of religion, government, or politics.

The ideological, the philosophical character of the "Wits'" interest in literature is further emphasized by their orientation in writing poetry from Lord Kames's *Elements of Criticism* (1762). Their profound debt, recently elucidated, to this Scottish philosopher is both characteristic and significant. Kames urged all prospective poets (and critics) to recognize "things as they are"; to accept "the common nature of man" as "invariable"; and to uphold a firm standard of "taste" for poetry and the other arts.[77] Through Kames the "Wits" became fascinated by the idea of an "internal sense," possessed by all men, which would be immediate in its judgments, and therefore independent of elaborate reasoning processes.[78] Thus they were interested in the "limitations of the human mind," and in the philosophical inwardness of literature. In a sense, this discipline enlarged their conception of the nature of poetry, but they were still far, if we think of the romantics, from a passion for literature for its own sake.

Nevertheless, in brief sittings the poetry of the "Connecticut

Wits" makes entertaining reading, from the idyllic scenes in Dwight's *Greenfield Hill* to the clever Dr. Lemuel Hopkins's "Epitaph on a Patient Killed by a Cancer Quack":

> Here lies a fool flat on his back,
> The victim of a Cancer Quack;
> Who lost his money and his life,
> By plaister, caustic, and by knife.
> The case was this—a pimple rose,
> South-east a little of his nose. . . .[79]

Humorous, satirical, or portentous, the lesser, intermittent "Wits," such as Richard Alsop, Elihu Hubbard Smith, or Theodore Dwight, still breathe the breath of life, even in their works of collaboration, *The Echo* and *The Anarchiad*.[80]

* * *

Of the major "Wits" John Trumbull was at once the eldest, the longest-lived, the most penetrative, and perhaps the least impervious to literature as an art. He was a true child of neoclassic theory, and though he experimented a little in satire, any real rebellion in his soul against standard forms he easily put down. Trumbull became our first master of the technique of satire, a province in which, as Poe later pointed out, Americans have never excelled.[81] He exposed the follies of mankind, with tarragon but also with decorum. Despite his Puritan upbringing and his thirty-one years in the nineteenth century, Trumbull practiced repeatedly this particular theory of eighteenth century poetry, the theory of the mock-epic and the burlesque. Moreover, he adjusted his trenchant couplets to the American scene. Barlow celebrated its misty glories; Trumbull ridiculed its visible absurdities.

Among the butts for Trumbull's shafts were his puerile college education at Yale, the New England town-meeting, the Tory squire in tar and feathers, and other angularities of the young republic, on which the satirist meditated as he studied law in the office of John Adams. *The Progress of Dulness* (1772–1773) was hampered by its misleading title and was eclipsed by *M'Fingal* (1776), Trumbull's masterpiece; the earlier poem satirized in three parts a dunce, a fop, and a coquette. A juvenile effort—Trumbull was hardly more than twenty when he composed it—this burlesque is less

"American" than the longer book. The half-educated Harriet Simper might as well be in London as in the country town of New Haven:

> "And what can mean your simple whim here
> To keep her poring on her primer?
> 'Tis quite enough for girls to know,
> If she can read a billet-deaux,
> Or write a line you'll understand
> Without an alphabet o'th'hand."[82]

The couplets are happy, but the target lacks sharpness of outline. Not so, in *M'Fingal*! The four lively cantos etch the passions of Revolutionary times. The dismal, ludicrous fate of the Squire lingers in the mind, and so do the nimble rhymes:

> No man e'er felt the halter draw,
> With good opinion of the law.[83]

By Trumbull's own confession the spirits of Swift and Churchill live again in *M'Fingal*,[84] but the long debates between the Squire and Honorius are indigenous. Sometimes in his treatment of the controversies between patriot and Tory Trumbull is playful, sometimes comic. Elsewhere in the poem he is tart to a degree surprising in one of his mild nature.[85] Yet he is always the intellectual master of his complicated material. He is practicing an amplification, which he had discussed somewhat in theory, of two types of burlesque.[86] Without the depth of Dryden, Trumbull remains, as our increasing regard for *M'Fingal* proves, a respectable, if imitative, American eighteenth century satirist.[87]

* * *

For his early poem, *America*, the learned Timothy Dwight studied intensively *Windsor Forest*.[88] Concerning the epic and the pastoral he must have cherished his own theories but he handed down to posterity, along with the formidable works themselves, no tangible definitions. He lacked apparently Trumbull's inquisitiveness concerning the current techniques in poetry. Perhaps he was too busy preaching. At any rate, his epics, satires, pastorals, and lyrics seem rooted, not in a loving study of these crafts, as in the case of Trumbull, but in the accepted vernacular. Without exhausting speculation about their purposes, he wrote stereotyped versions of epic or satire. Indeed, for Dwight the laws of poetry were as fixed as those of staid, old Connecticut, in which he counselled Federalism, or of the pulpit, from which he thundered Calvinism, or of Yale College, of which he was for many years the forceful but somewhat pachyderm President. Dwight's literary career, which began at the age of seventeen with essays in imitation of the *Spectator*, ended, it may be said, with the posthumous publication of *Theology: Explained and Defended, in a Series of Sermons* (1818–1819). Dwight was always defending the established. If he did not do so officially for poetry, it was probably because he thought it unnecessary. Poetry meant, he was sure, the heroic couplet and sensible discourse on religion, on politics, and on the American countryside.

Even in *The Conquest of Canäan* (1785), even in these "eleven dreadful books of conventional rhymed pentameters,"[89] Dwight's interest is diverted toward the modern American man in his struggle to found a nation worthy of the Enlightenment. His long descriptions of human felicity in this new "promised land" are most eloquent in *Greenfield Hill*[90] (1794), his best poem by reason of its verbal engravings of rural New England. In this, and in *The Triumph of Infidelity* (1788), in which he brushes aside Voltaire and other skeptics, he draws contrasting pictures; he counterpoints that unfortunate man who knows neither true religion nor this Utopian America with the happy dweller in the New England village. Indeed, about Dwight's religious and patriotic gusto there is something overwhelming. As he declaims in his poetry his religious or social convictions, he resembles a high wind.

Buffeted by these poetic blasts, we turn with relief to the comparative quiet of Dwight's pastoral scenes, so reminiscent of English models, and so typical, on the whole, of the poetic practice we are now studying:

> "Such, such, my children, is the dismal cot,
> Where drowsy Sloth receives her wretched lot:
> But O how different is the charming cell,
> Where Industry and Virtue love to dwell!
>
> "Beyond that hillock, topp'd with scatter'd trees,
> That meet, with freshest green, the hastening breeze,
> . . . .

A female Worthy lives; and all the poor
Can point the way to her sequester'd door.
. . . .

    "Small is her house; but fill'd with stores of good;
Good, earn'd with toil, and with delight bestow'd.
In the clean cellar, rang'd in order neat,
Gay-smiling Plenty boasts her casks of meat,
Points, to small eyes, the bins where apples glow,
And marks her cyder-butts, in stately row.
Her granary, fill'd with harvest's various pride,
Still sees the poor man's bushel laid aside;
Here swells the flaxen, there the fleecy store,
And the long wood-pile mocks the winter's power:
White are the swine; the poultry plump and large;
For every creature thrives, beneath her charge."[91]

*   *   *

Surely for a kind of grandiose utility few poets have ever surpassed these "Connecticut Wits." After the poultry, Dwight, never a master of the unexpected, hymns the furniture, the pewter vessels, and the washed coverlet on the bed. This solemn versification of household possessions, this kitchen poetry, as it might be called, is less offensive when it escapes from the humorless Dwight to Joel Barlow, who when in cheerful vein was not unworthy of the Augustan tradition of light verse. For Mrs. Washington he celebrated in whimsical mood, while he was living in Savoy, the joys of a simple American dish. There is gaiety in this poem, *The Hasty Pudding* (1796), with its gustatory climax:

    There is a choice in spoons. Though small appear
The nice distinction, yet to me 'tis clear.
The deep-bowled Gallic spoon, contrived to scoop
In ample draughts the thin diluted soup.[92]

So continues this pleasant nonsense in verse. Barlow's mind had more flexibility than Dwight's, more subtlety than Humphreys's (not a bold claim), and more courage than Trumbull's, as his dramatic life-story demonstrated. Army chaplain in the Revolution, lawyer, business-man, traveller, and resident for long periods in Europe, he was in his middle years reborn in all the liberalisms of England and France. He became the friend of Horne Tooke, and for his book, *Advice to the Privileged Orders* (1793), he enjoyed the praise of the British statesman, Charles Fox. He died in Poland, during Napoleon's invasion of Russia; it was a strange ending for the career commenced in far-away Connecticut.

Throughout his busy life Barlow wrote poetry, from *The Prospect of Peace*, his juvenile poem at Yale, with its significant subtitle, *A Political Composition*, to the prodigious epic which for so many years absorbed his leisure hours. The final version of this protracted masterpiece, which took initial form in 1787, in *The Vision of Columbus*, did not appear until five years before his death. *The Columbiad* (1807), so vast that few have read it and so violent that Hawthorne suggested the accompaniments of artillery, thunder, and lightning, was an epical vision of the future of all the Americas.[93] Like Barlow's other poetry, it was a sounding board for his own political ideas. Less attracted than Trumbull to satire or than Dwight to themes of religion, Barlow evidently thought of verse as a medium for his own liberal concepts of man's destiny. The popular poetic forms he accepted without question; the differences from his friends center in his Jacobinical ideas and in his unconquerable delight in social gospels.

Thus Barlow's poetry is really a deposition of his humanitarian philosophy. His natural wit, revealed by *The Hasty Pudding*, he suppressed, to argue concerning the common man. Certain sentences in the preface to *The Columbiad*, however boring to modern readers, reveal not only Barlow's characteristic use of the epic, but also his fine, clear sympathies as a human being:

> The real object [he says] of the poem embraces a larger scope; it is to inculcate the love of rational liberty, and to discountenance the deleterious passion for violence and war; to show that on the basis of the republican principle all good morals, as well as good government and hopes of permanent peace, must be founded.[94]

Viewed in the light of Barlow's life-purposes, the ancient jokes on the size and rhetoric of *The Columbiad* lose their virtue. Imbedded in it is Barlow's dream of the political and social destiny of man.

*   *   *

To discuss in detail other individual "Wits" would be to transgress the limits of their place in this chapter. It would also show the practice of eighteenth century poetic theory at its worst, in watery versions of the honored forms we have been studying. Nevertheless, in spite of idiosyncrasies of craftsmanship or of personality; these minor "Wits" are likely to remain important in any record of American poetry. The sardonic Dr. Lemuel Hopkins, enemy of humbug in medicine or politics; the amiable Richard Alsop, learned in Continental languages; the democracy-hating Theodore Dwight; the sonorous David Humphreys, friend of George Washington and breeder of merino sheep; all these implemented the poetic theories which now, on the eve of the next century, though they were marked for decline, were still mighty. These lesser American poets also illustrated, if without too much talent, the lofty concepts of Dryden and Pope.

For, whereas the exaggeration of seventeenth century principles seemed to bring in its train the harsh line, the thorny metaphor, the extravagant emotion, so now the exaggeration of eighteenth century modes fostered the rhetorical and the vapid. In this regard one poet is particularly vulnerable. David Humphreys, with a distinguished career as a soldier, diplomat, and farmer, turned a slender talent for meter into such indiscretions as *A Poem Addressed to the Armies of the United States of America* (1780), another entitled *A Poem on the Happiness of America* (1786), and one called *A Poem on Industry* (1794). The story that Humphreys in his room at Mount Vernon sometimes started from his bed at night to declaim poetry must not be taken too lightly; the anecdote is not inconsistent with his oratorical standards for poetry.[95] He thought it a craft no more demanding than prose or formal conversation with his "dear General," George Washington. He found it, in fact, appropriate for daily records; he could describe a meeting with a fellow wit in this fashion:

> Some days elaps'd, I jogg'd quite brave on
> And found my *Trumbull* at New-Haven.[96]

Or he could invoke in verse the vocation in which he was really a master:

> Thee, Agriculture! source of every joy.[97]

* * *

Thus the theory that poetry should describe the reasoning man reaches a sad ultimate in Humphreys and in some verse of the

other "Wits." The Philadelphia Group was, as we have seen, in-
clined to muse a little on a mysterious relationship between man
and nature. However faintly, they seem now to have anticipated
the romantic poetry not then so many years distant. With similar
wisdom after the event, we might acclaim other forerunners, in
particular Philip Freneau, so admired by Thomas Campbell and
Walter Scott. It may be so; in a few of Freneau's lyrics appears a
mood of longing undiscoverable in Hopkinson, Barlow, or Timothy
Dwight. Freneau's distaste for the solemn patriotism of a *Green-
field Hill* or the heavy humanitarianism of a *Columbiad* may be
inferred from the subjects of his poems. Yes, his perception of the
changing phases of nature may be regarded as the first notes of a
more passionate music. In any case, his sensuous feeling for the
natural world, and the fresh quality of some half-dozen lyrics have
persuaded critics to accord him this honor of precursor. Was he
America's first romantic poet?

Possibly. Yet the conclusion that Freneau was essentially a
transitional poet should be neither hasty nor unqualified. His
restlessness under Augustan rules finds, after all, no complete ex-
pression even in his best lyrics, such as "The Wild Honey Suckle"
or "The Indian Burying Ground." Moreover, in his verse we are
forever confronting lines, extended passages, techniques, and ways
of thought which intimate less his apostasy than his unswerving
loyalty. Evidently, until his death in the second decade of the next
century, he relied upon "thrice-happy Dryden" and on "heav'nly
Pope." If he had a pre-romantic love of nature, he controlled it; he
balanced it with ideas and language which would have done honor
to these literary dictators. For instance, he begins his delightful
poem, "The Power of Fancy," in this fashion:

> Wakeful, vagrant, restless thing,
> Ever wandering on the wing. . . .[98]

Yet a few lines later he is on his knees before the universe of the
Enlightenment:

> Ah! what is all this mighty whole,
> These suns and stars that round us roll!
> What are they all, where'er they shine,
> But Fancies of the Power Divine!
> What is this globe, these lands and seas,

And heat, and cold, and flowers, and trees,
And life, and death, and beast, and man,
And time—that with the sun began—
But thoughts on reason's scale combin'd,
Ideas of the Almighty Mind![99]

One fact is sure. At heart Freneau was a poet, and not, like the "Wits," a man of action who fabricated verse. Early in life he refers to himself as "unfit for cities and the noisy throng";[100] and he resolves that in poetry he will "center every wish."[101] Such determinations were different indeed from Timothy Dwight's; and his temper differs, too, in its spirit of dedication, from that of the Philadelphia Group. Their rebellion, such as it was, was not toward a consecration to the Muse but toward her greater sophistication, and, perhaps, toward a more romantic view of nature.

Sometimes the youthful Freneau reminds us of William Cullen Bryant, not only in his desire to make nature more concrete, but in his dismay at the forces which threaten to expel him from his world of dreams into the fierce American life of his era. In this involuntary exile from his art, he, too, anticipated this recurring experience of the poet in the republic. A Whig both by temperament and by his early associations at Princeton, he was drafted into a war of vituperation. At least a third of all Freneau's writing belongs to satire, shallow and bitter, such as "George the Third's Soliloquy" or *The British Prison-Ship*; and at least three-fourths of his poetry bears in line or stanza the stamp of his years as a sailor, a prisoner of war, a politician, a journalist, or a bitter enemy of Britain and Hesse.

Most of Freneau's political verse deserves its oblivion; confined in the usual forms, it is hardly better, except for its convincing fury, than the mediocre satirical passages written by the "Wits." In any case, as sheer satire, much of it is inferior to that of the incisive Trumbull; it is, indeed, often mere objurgation:

From a kingdom that bullies, and hectors, and swears,
We send up to heaven our wishes and prayers
That we, disunited, may freemen be still,
And Britain go on—to be damned if she will.[102]

The redeeming quality in Freneau's doggerel is connected with the occasional flashes of reality from his own life; he himself had suffered the horrors of a British prison ship. His other poetry, which cannot be separated too sharply from his verse of the Revolution, depends upon experiences equally authentic: his repeated stays in the soft climate of the West Indies; his meditations (as in his Poesque "House of Night") on death; or his knowledge of the American Indian, which ultimately produced his finest lyric.

In this poem, "The Indian Burying Ground," as in "The Wild Honey Suckle" and in a few others, there is use of native flowers and of native natural objects. In this way, also, Freneau anticipated Bryant. He speaks of the katydid, the whippoorwill,—not to mention Virginia tobacco! Nevertheless, in the very first line of "The Indian Burying Ground" occurs an allusion to "the learned" of past ages and in the last stanza appears a reference to "Reason." And meanwhile, his familiar eighteenth century rhyme schemes seem to deny any real emancipation. In this poem and in others, such as "The Indian Student," Freneau might almost be writing as an eighteenth century English visitor to our shores:

> From Susquehanna's farthest springs
> Where savage tribes pursue their game,
> (His blanket tied with yellow strings,)
> A shepherd of the forest came.[103]

For these reasons, as we conclude this part of our story, it becomes evident that Freneau, though freer in spirit than other poets of his time, still belongs to the eighteenth century. Well-grounded in the classics, he translates Horace; few of his poems lack a brocade of mythological allusions. In the Bermudas he sees "woodland nymphs," in Jamaica "sultry Phoebus," and in Santa Cruz he recalls Ulysses and the lotus-eaters. Throughout these long descriptions of the American tropics flourish the clichés of Augustan poetry. Graceful and tranquil poet he was, compared with the noisy Connecticut "Wits," but, like them, he wrote under the spell of the clear Augustan sunlight rather than of the romantic dawn.[104] Indeed, the history of Freneau's verse furnishes final evidence of the extraordinary fidelity of American poets to those neoclassic principles with which in this second chapter we have been primarily concerned.

CHAPTER III

THE POET OF EARLY ROMANTICISM

A N A C T of reason, exercising and dignifying the individual mind which performs it, may at the same time stimulate it to a more adventurous way of thought. Perhaps by analogy the Enlightenment, though it stressed reason and abhorred excess, set the stage for a bolder drama,—that of the imagination, that, in other words, of Romanticism. What is this? No final answer exists. The present book makes no attempt to define it; it does not analyze Puritanism, the Enlightenment, Romanticism, or Transcendentalism. These captions serve merely as convenient guides for our study of the development of American poetry, in theory and practice. The dangers of attempting definitions of romanticism have been demonstrated again and again;[1] and at this moment a new generation of scholars still tries to snare this elusive bird.[2]

Nevertheless, though the word may take on nearly any meaning its user may desire, we cannot abandon it. Whatever reservations come to mind, it still makes sense to refer, for normal purposes of study, to, let us say, the "neoclassic" poetry of Timothy Dwight or the "romantic" poetry of Poe. For in the day of the latter, at least by 1840, the individual had embraced new outlooks concerning religion, society, or the arts. Hence the prevalence of these fresh patterns justifies us in saying, even as we realize the multiple meanings of the word in every province of life in the nineteenth century, that the age of neoclassicism had yielded to the age of romanticism.

In fact, in Newtonian science, in deism, in kindred fashions of thought lay the embryo of what we call inexactly romanticism.[3] Beginning, perhaps, as a protest against reason's claims to be the sole interpreter of life, it infused itself into nearly every activity of man, with ever-increasing fervor. In interpretations of the past men of letters and even historians inclined toward "imagination" as their guide; their comparative silence concerning "reason" is suggestive. If we desire external causes and consequences connected with romanticism, we shall, of course, pause over the Renaissance, the Reformation, the French Revolution, or over Hartley, Locke, Rousseau, and Kant (to mention only a few of the high priests). We can then ponder the complexity of this pattern both in society and in solitude, both in the outward and inward life of man. We shall be unable to define precisely what happened either in origins or development, but we shall see, in any case, man emerging from the law-ridden eighteenth century into a more subjective and more imaginative view of the universe and of himself.

This story, with all its intricate crosscurrents, is too long to be chronicled here. We understand, too, of course, that this so-called "romantic" impulse has always existed in every age and in every country, but that its triumph, so to speak, occurred in the nineteenth century after those developments which we have just studied, in the eighteenth.[4] In the more recent century it became in all its phases a movement, that is, a conscious struggle against neoclassic modes of thought. Presently its creeds dominated men's minds as strongly as had, a century or so before, the different ideology of the Enlightenment. Through that sensitive seismograph, literature, we have perceived, for example, in the poetry of the English Thomson or the American Freneau, the faint tremors of new creations. Now, at the beginning of the nineteenth century, poets of early romanticism, as we somewhat arbitrarily call them, enjoyed a release, like that of the English poets, from eighteenth century orthodoxies. In both England and America delay and hostility impeded the growth of the new faith[5] but by the fourth decade in men's minds were new assumptions; the ideas of Kant or Shelley had become as credible (and more satisfying) than those of Newton or Pope. With a cultural lag this was to be so also in America. Against the background of these new, exciting criteria were to appear such poems as "Monument Mountain," "The Belfry of Bruges," or "The Raven."

The vitality of romanticism in the many fields of human knowledge lay primarily in this use of the imagination, instead of the reason, in this longing for what might be instead of what is, in this dream of the infinite, instead of the finite. Through the imagination man could cross the borders of the unknown.[6] To separate the inward impulse from certain outward consequences (such as the movement of humanitarianism) is no less dangerous than the inclusive definitions which have betrayed so many historians and critics. It is too simple to call romanticism, as does M. Brunetière, an emancipation of the "ego,"[7] but to attempt much more is to cease to define; it is merely to list characteristics. Our dictionaries and histories of literature abound in ambitious, interminable sentences which hope to bind within their limits these component parts of romanticism.[8] Yet always, like the genie, it escapes from the bottle!

Probably we should all try, at one time or another, to catalogue for ourselves these traits; to attempt to comprehend the chemistry of this fluid body. We may not be able to fasten on a central characteristic, but we can learn to recognize the parts in this baffling amalgam: medievalism, love of nature, longing for the remote, primitivism, supernaturalism, the freedoms of society and the individual, and so on.[9] If we cannot name the dish, we may at least know the ingredients. Or we may play with inadequate but provocative contrasts of the two ways of thought, the "classic" and the "romantic," as in this passage written by an American while looking back upon our literature of the nineteenth century:

> For general purposes [he says] one would not go far wrong who should include under the term "classic" that sort of human impulse which reached its highest form in the fine arts of Greece, and under the term "romantic" that which most nearly approached realization in the art and the literature of mediæval Europe. The essence of classic art is perhaps that the artist realises the limits of his conception, and within those limits endeavours to make his expression completely beautiful. The essence of the romantic spirit is that the artist, whatever his conception, is always aware of the infinite mysteries which lie beyond it.[10]

* * *

"Infinite mysteries which lie beyond!" The phrase is not inapplicable to English poetry of the first half of the century, whether we think of Wordsworth's "Lines Composed a Few Miles above Tintern Abbey" or of Keats's "The Eve of St. Agnes." Some poets, like Rossetti, were retrospective, living again in the Middle

Ages. We think of Byron trailing "the pageant of his bleeding heart" through distant scenes, or Coleridge fancying painted ships upon painted oceans or sights "to dream of, not to tell." Still others, such as Keats or Shelley, lost themselves in the color of a flower or in the spiritual or political destiny of man.[11] Yet in all these categories no "limits" were set; nothing was settled by reason; all these poets were sensitive to the "infinite mysteries," to the unseen behind the thing seen. In English literature this state of mind, dynamic and, in time, self-conscious, created "schools" and "movements," which, though our own circles of writers were still relatively weak and inarticulate, affected American poetry deeply.[12] On both sides of the Atlantic reason and the heroic couplet qualified these new insanities; one remembers Byron's satires, Hawthorne's classic unities in *The Scarlet Letter*, or Poe's interest in the science of Newton and the thought of Thomas Jefferson.[13] Nevertheless, before the turn of the half-century mark "the mysteries" ruled our poets.

By its very charter of liberty America might seem an excellent proving-ground for a movement which stressed freedom for the individual. And in some ways it was, as we shall see. In other particulars it was a barren acreage for the basic romantic impulses.[14] The championship of the downtrodden, the zeal for political freedom, so fiercely pursued in Europe, had at this time relatively less significance in prosperous, democratic America. The antiquarian or the medievalist would find little material within a country which was years later to be denounced as sterile in this regard by both Nathaniel Hawthorne and Henry James.[15] The wanderer, Irving, and the traveling scholar, Longfellow, seem to be exceptions, but their nostalgia for Europe merely re-emphasizes the cultural blanks in their own country. On the other hand, the romantic's passion for natural scenery was both satisfied and stimulated here; Balzac acclaimed Cooper's idealized lakes and forests as "sublime."[16] Thus in America romantic impulses were to be both restricted and enlarged. The pattern became, finally, special, individual, as unique in its way as the philosophic romanticism of Germany. Is it, then, possible to say a little more of "American" romanticism?

In general, American romanticism reflected the level of the country's culture during these early decades: it was less sophisticated, less learned, less philosophic, less esoteric than the romanticism of Europe.[17] A certain distinguished historian of English romanticism who frankly centered his studies in its medievalism[18] would have applied with difficulty this selective process to American romanticism. The American reader was friendly toward the medieval past of Europe, and even a little wistful; Longfellow's poetry on these themes was popular. The day had not arrived when Whitman was to denounce "feudalism"[19] and to transfer the romantic's allegiance from the past to the future; when Mark Twain was to express in volume after volume his hatred of the medieval era.[20] Nevertheless, the tournaments of Walter Scott, the Alhambra of Irving or the Albrecht Dürer of Longfellow seemed apart from the main stream of the republic's growth; in the nation's past were no crusaders to Jerusalem, no Moorish palaces, no red-roofed German villages. Such writers faced toward Europe.[21] Whatever was to be original in American romanticism would not stem from medievalism.[22]

Partly from our confused attitude toward the past, partly from the limitations of our materials, partly from our moral inhibitions, American romanticism developed a peculiar, hesitant quality—a mixture of imitation and nationalism.[23] During the first half-century many critics and poets remained diffident concerning native subjects. "We want," admitted Doctor Channing, "a remote antiquity."[24] "No shadow," said Hawthorne forty-five years later, as if continuing the Doctor's lament, "no antiquity, no mystery, no picturesque and gloomy wrong."[25] Everywhere reverberates the same dirge in journals or magazines, in essays, stories, or verse.[26] James Abraham Hillhouse, a poet of some stature in his day, admired by Coleridge, had romantic tastes, but the subject for his most ambitious poem was the story of Hadad in the Bible:

> Our history [he remarked sadly] is allied to the calmness and plainness of intellect, rather than to the hurry and splendour of imagination: it is distinguished rather for an inflexible adherence to principles, than for a vast variety of brilliant achievements.[27]

As for those barbaric peoples who antedated the white man in North America, romance could not draw sustenance from "the mummery of aboriginal superstition."[28]

Nevertheless, in the frantic search for the materials for a national literature others opposed this rejection of our own "antiquity";

these believers in our past challenged Cooper's assertion that America offered "no annals for the historian."[29] In 1828, in a half-contemptuous estimate of his countrymen, the novelist had declared that there was "no costume for the peasant, (there is scarcely a peasant at all,) no wig for the judge, no baton for the general, no diadem for the chief magistrate."[30] Cooper did not crave these adornments, but he was depressed by what Irving called in a private letter "the all pervading commonplace which is the curse of our country."[31] On the other hand, nationalist writers acclaimed the unwritten sagas of the Indian nations. Were there not, also unwritten, the epics of conquest and exploration by the English, French, and Spanish? Were there not "ancient legends and visionary prophecies, . . . in abundance and endless variety?"[32] Were there not the Revolution and the settling of the West? Possibly the fault lay not in the past but in the poet himself, timid and anglophile? In fact, even Irving thought Thomas Campbell's *Gertrude of Wyoming* a reminder to American poets of the richness of this past. Throughout this prolonged controversy we feel the poet's insecurity concerning his materials, a state of mind characteristic of adolescence in literature.

Similar confusions clouded the American poet's view of the supernatural.[33] Charles Brockden Brown transferred the techniques of Mrs. Radcliffe to an American setting; Poe borrowed from the German tale of horror; and Hawthorne, perhaps half-ironic, employed the Gothic tradition in his novel of the dark, historic house of Salem.[34] Ethical expressions of the romantic impulse, such as feminism or abolition, seemed to run wild in America, but uncertainty is visible again in our poets' treatment of nature. How could "the great mother" as Emerson called her, possibly inspire the poet if she lacked the associations of the past? Concerning nature the poet might, indeed, write descriptive poetry,

> but without the traditional associations connected with the stronger features of Nature, even in the old world, what could be made of them? . . . It is the magic of association that fits every thing for the poets' hand; and at this moment, and it will perhaps be the case for years to come, more poetry is to be made out of the humblest hillock upon the surface of the long inhabited regions of the other continent, than out of the whole American chain of Apalaches, Alleganies and Andes.[35]

John Bristed, also dismayed, stated the problem more succinctly:

> The aspect of nature, in the United States, presents magnificence
> and beauty in all profusion; but hill and dale, and wood and stream,
> are not alone sufficient to breathe the inspirations of poetry, unless
> seconded by the habits and manners, the feelings, taste and char-
> acter of the inhabitants.[36]

Yet in their response to nature is the glory, if such it may be
called, of some of these first American poets of romanticism. Al-
though it lacked memories, that is, what Emerson was to refer to
as the envelopment of great actions, in another way American
landscape offered the poet far more than the lakes of England or
the mountains of Switzerland. Cooper was hardly fair to his own
materials when he declared: "There is scarcely an ore which con-
tributes to the wealth of the author, that is found, here, in veins
as rich as in Europe."[37] This romancer had not yet given us his
far-flung panorama of forest, plain, and inland sea. It was this
extravagance, this "primitivism," so to speak, of our nature, so
often associated with thoughts of elemental man, which bestowed
upon American romanticism a kind of spaciousness. If in the fol-
lowing passage Hillhouse is rhetorical, he speaks truth about this
particular quality:

> True, we have no mouldering ruins of feudal power, and none of
> the romantic legends which linger round them. . . . Our forests
> breathe upon us the freshness of primeval nature. . . . the grand
> eternal forms of nature. Vast, solitary and sublime, pressing on
> the mind the symbols of creative power, rather than mementos of
> departed human pride.[38]

Regarding nature in this fashion, it became easy for the romantic
poet in America to interest himself in primitive peoples. Declar-
ing that the Indians in council and in war resembled the ancient
Greeks, William Tudor called for an American epic.[39] Such a tend-
ency was, among our men of letters, far from widespread, but the
sentimental mood first encountered in Freneau's lyrics on the In-
dian[40] was now, in the early nineteenth century, strongly accented.
For both novelists and poets the red man became a favorite theme,
in Cooper's *The Last of the Mohicans*, in Bryant's "Monument
Mountain," or in Longfellow's *Song of Hiawatha*. In fact, as me-
dievalism seems, after all, an important element in English roman-

ticism, so this primitivism of nature and this primitivism of
man, whether concerned with Leatherstocking, the Indian, or the
negro, may prove to be an enduring quality in the romanticism
of America.

*   *   *

All the American poets of the first decades of the century reveal,
with varying emphases, these identical romantic interests. Not
only in the three or four selected for special consideration, Bryant,
Whittier, Longfellow, and Poe, but in dozens of others recur these
preoccupations with the past: with supernaturalism, with nature,
with the primitive dwellers on the Continent. In all are excesses
of feeling (ecstasy or melancholy); in all is this sense of the emanci-
pation of the "ego." In most of them, although the eighteenth
century prosody did not yield easily, are corresponding freedoms
in verse forms.[41] Few definitions of theory as concrete as those of
Bryant or Poe were formulated by these lesser poets, but in a letter
of Fitz-Greene Halleck or in a preface by James Gates Percival[42]
we discover a search for new principles and an ever-growing dis-
taste for neoclassicism. Thus both public and authors were in-
tensely interested in the world of fancy created by the youthful
poet, Joseph Rodman Drake, in his dream of fairy lore, *The Cul-
prit Fay*.[43] We should examine for a moment these minor poets who
have been outlived by Bryant, Longfellow, and Poe.

The medievalism, for example, which secured a hold on Ameri-
can romanticism, is well illustrated, though less distinguished in
expression than Longfellow's or Poe's, by one of the Knicker-
bocker Group, a coterie violently opposed to neoclassicism and all
its works. This was Fitz-Greene Halleck, a violent enemy of "reason"
and of its dead hand on poetry. Halleck wrote charming satiric
verse. In other ways, too, he was a disciple of Lord Byron, and it
is both amusing and suggestive to learn how, on receiving the
news of his master's death, he "walked up and down the drawing-
room wringing his hands, saying, . . . 'What a terrible loss to
literature!' "[44]

At the same time there can be no doubt of Halleck's sincerity
in demanding for his village Muse "the vision and the faculty
divine."[45] Poetry, he cried,

can be explained in a word: it's simply the opposite of reason! Reason is based on fact; and fact is not poetry. A poet has nothing to do with the facts of things, for he must continually deny them![46]

In this connection Halleck quoted from Wordsworth's "Song at the Feast of Brougham Castle":

> Armor, rusting on his walls
> On the blood of Clifford calls;—
> 'Quell the Scott!' exclaims the lance—
> 'Bear me to the heart of France!'
> Is the longing of the shield.[47]

He then added his own comment: "There! was ever anything more irrational than the lance exclaiming and the shield longing?—but what poetry it is!"[48] It is difficult to agree. Yet "Alnwick Castle" is only one of Halleck's poems reflecting his pleasure, this time touched with satire, in the pageantry of the Middle Ages.[49] Thus practice conformed with theory.

Joseph Rodman Drake, like his friend Halleck, a lover of witty verse and the inspirer by his early death of the latter's finest lyric,[50] moved easily, without bequeathing us precise theories, in the same world. In his lyric on the stars and stripes he could dwell fondly on a medieval word,

> The milky baldric of the skies.[51]

Usually, however, Drake's talent was for the playful, the lightly imaginative, as in *The Culprit Fay*, rather than for the somewhat theatrical world of Halleck.

Drake had sharp eyes: he saw fairies in the Hudson River countryside. Such was the corrupting influence of romanticism! Meanwhile, James Gates Percival, found beauty not in "the blue, arrowy Rhone, nor Leman's lake,"[52] but in his native Lake Seneca. In the same fashion other minor romantics, such as Charles Fenno Hoffman, Nathaniel Parker Willis, George P. Morris, Samuel Woodworth, or Robert C. Sands idealized local scenes. Halleck's *Fanny*, a Byronic satire, appeared in 1819; Percival's *Poems* in 1821. By the time Drake died, a year earlier, although the ideas of the Enlightenment and neoclassic verse were far from extinct, American poetry was really committed to its new future.

What underlying concepts shaped this pattern in which were grounded also the greater poets, Bryant, Longfellow, and Poe?

We have already perceived that all the ideas and moods of European romanticism found some acceptance in America. In addition, these were amplified to include our own scenery, our own primitive man, the Indian, or even, as in the case of Longfellow, our domestic life. The referent of all this interest was evidently the *imagination*, the emancipation of the "ego," instead of, as in the eighteenth century, the laws of Newton and "reason." Yet the peculiar American flavor of these romantics, evident, also, in the work of Bryant or Longfellow (but not in that of Poe),[53] is, I think, of another kind.

This quality, somewhat difficult to define, may be described in over-simplified fashion as *moral*. The romantic poets of Cambridge or of Concord (Longfellow or Emerson)[54] were in tone essentially religious as befitted the descendants of the Puritans, and in varying degrees (in contrast to Byron and Shelley) this temper entered into all our early nineteenth century verse. Thus Halleck was a chastened Byron and Drake a mild Keats (a conjunction which angered the English critics) not wholly because they were inferior in talent. Somehow their verse emanated ethical and religious feeling; all these poets were sensitive to what Emerson called "the moral sentiment."[55]

Only the boldest critic would attempt to trace the origins of this temper to precise causes, to, for example, Puritanism, to the peculiar history of American Protestantism, to the still living influence of eighteenth century moralism, or to mere propriety in its revulsion from the cruder standards of our society. In any case, this relish for the "moral sentiment" mildews the freshness of these early romantic poets. Perhaps it should be added that this "sentiment" affected not merely our writing but all our arts. Captain Marryat remembered particularly from his visit to America the story that Governor Everett of Boston had, with admirable modesty, hung his fine cast of the Apollo Belvidere with drapery.[56] So in this poetry there is something depressingly decorous: it offers sentiment but no passion; the sensuous abandon of Byron and Keats and the intellectual freedom of Shelley are unhappily absent.

James Gates Percival (who deserves a fresh biography) displayed in his eccentric life an air of rebellion, but in his writing this intransigence was limited to a daring theory of prosody anticipatory of Whitman.[57] The sentimentality of his poetry is in harmony with his language in his brief statements of theory. We must endure the rhetoric in the following passage for what it reveals of this "moral" alloy in American romanticism:

> The poet . . . [says Percival] gives to his conceptions a visible form of beauty or of power, and animates them with a fire from heaven. . . . He takes you to the retirement of sensibility . . . and plays upon the springs which call forth those feelings of happy sorrow, which move us in our sympathies with others, which are always delightful, because they seem to us holy. . . . Every tear that is shed then is to us a treasure; for it flows from a fountain in which we imagine angels might wash and be purer. Even when he becomes the hierophant of nature, and leads us to contemplate the great principles of our being, when he is simply didactic, and his great object is the display of philosophic truth, he does not depart from his peculiar character.[58]

Poe was right; these early poets were corroded by "the heresy of *The Didactic.*"[59] Only he, directly, and Emerson, obliquely, opposed didacticism in American poetry before the appearance of *Leaves of Grass* in 1855.

* * *

Percival's principles are vague enough, but they are hardly more abstract than Bryant's theories of poetry at which, after this background in the lesser poets, we now arrive. Having read Halleck or Percival, we shall understand that his sentimental and moral concepts did not represent an isolated attitude. As a matter-of-fact, Bryant was our first poet to set down a substantial body of poetic theory. As early as 1811, when only seventeen years old, he was at work on his mildly iconoclastic essay, "On the Use of Trisyllabic Feet in Iambic Verse" (1819). A year before its publication he had prefaced a review by a discussion of American verse; and in April, 1826, he delivered four lectures on the nature of poetry.[60] In addition, he supplemented these many pages of explicit statement with further ideas in his literary criticism and with pungent, incidental comments, such as his famous confession to Richard Henry Dana after reading the *Lyrical Ballads*: "A thousand springs seemed to gush up at once in his heart, and the face of nature, of a sudden, to change into a strange freshness and life."[61] In his reading of Wordsworth and also in his awareness of Byron some of Bryant's poetic principles took lasting form.[62]

During the fifteen years (1811–1826) which established the char-
acter of Bryant's poetic theories we may follow his development
from a kind of boyish rage at neoclassic rules[63] to a tedious analysis
of originality and imitation in verse.[64] Evidently weaned away from
current fashions during his writing of "Thanatopsis" by his pleas-
ure in Blair, Cowper, and Thomson,[65] he attacked in this early
essay the hidebound "Connecticut Wits." He denounced, in
particular, the

> lofty, measured, declamatory manner—an artificial elevation of style,
> from which it is impossible to rise or descend without abruptness
> and violence, and which allows just as much play and freedom to
> the faculties of the writer as a pair of stilts allows the body. The
> imagination is confined to one trodden circle, doomed to the chains
> of a perpetual mannerism, and condemned to tinkle the same eter-
> nal tune with its fetters.[66]

Although his first great poem was in blank verse, and although he
admired Pope, Bryant was soon alienated from eighteenth century
standards; and on the foundation of this repudiation he began to
build his own theories. The direction these were to take is sug-
gested by another reason for his dislike of the Augustans: "The
heart," he said, "is rarely addressed."[67] He determined to speak
directly to the emotions.

For by "the heart," a cherished word among these romantics,
Bryant meant the emotions. In his lecture, "On the Nature of
Poetry," his distinctions between the "imagination" and "the heart"
seem artificial, and no clearer than his definition of the "luminous
style," another principle in his poetic creed.[68] To understand his
theories, more articulate than Longfellow's and less extravagant
than Poe's, we must, I think, study both the Scottish rhetoricians[69]
and also his guarded use of romantic passion as "emotion." Po-
etry does, he admits, reach the "understanding," but he exhorts
the reader to recognize a far deeper function. It "addresses the
passions and the imagination"; "strong feeling is always a sure
guide"; "it speaks a language which reaches the heart";[70] and so
on, endlessly. These ideas suggest Byron, but Bryant's "emotion"
permits no excess of any kind. It tolerates neither the meta-
physical gymnastics of Donne nor the "over-languaged"[71] richness
of Keats nor the "pomp of words"[72] by which Bryant thought Pope
tried to make the trivial resemble the noble. Closer to Wordsworth

than Byron, Bryant at the same time reminds us of familiar eight-
eenth century attitudes. He praises emotion, but we need not fear
that it will get out of hand.

Bryant's emotions, then, in poetry seem to have an inlay of
reason, an infusion of "understanding." He would

> .... clothe in words of flame
> Thoughts that shall live within the general mind![73]

This is to say that the emotions express themselves not in longing
for the Middle Ages, for the exotic, or the remote, but in "natural
objects, in the vicissitudes of human life . . . and the relations of
man to man."[74] Whether or not this passage echoes Wordsworth,
it characterizes the data, at least in theory, for Bryant's own poetry.
Other materials, again in theory, he found in nature; he would medi-
tate on human life in its relation to nature and describe them
both in a "luminous style."[75] The curb to the "emotions" is, of
course, as in the other poets, including Longfellow, the "moral
sentiment,"—a phrase which he himself uses twice in the following
passage on poetry and the natural world:

> Among the most remarkable of the influences of poetry is the
> exhibition of those analogies and correspondences which it beholds
> between the things of the moral and of the natural world. I refer
> to its adorning and illustrating each by the other—infusing a moral
> sentiment into natural objects, and bringing images of visible beauty
> and majesty to heighten the effect of moral sentiment.[76]

The passage, looking backward to Swedenborg and forward to
"Language" and "Discipline," the two sections dealing with this
analogy in Emerson's *Nature* (1836), really labels Bryant's poetic
principles as religious and ethical. As we shall see, several phases
of practice in Bryant's poetry receive in his manifestoes no con-
sideration, such as, to mention only two, his interest in supernatu-
ralism[77] and primitivism. Nevertheless, his key theories reside in
the passages just quoted. These excerpts enlarge, also, the meaning
of his word "luminous," concerning which as applied to style he
is far from specific. He meant, to be sure, clarity of expression,
but his emphasis on the "moral sentiment" hints at more than
lucidity of meaning. He was evidently thinking of the light of
moral truth,—a shining suffusion throughout his poetry of these
high concepts, in clear and faithful language.

Bryant denies that he advocates "didactic" poetry, but his un-
flagging talk of "light," of the "moral sentiment," of the union of
"truth and beauty," of "the heart," or of the "luminous" style ren-
ders his disclaimers irritating. To the modern reader this is apt to
be a tiresome body of theory, not free from contradiction, and we
must again remind ourselves that Bryant belonged to two centu-
ries. Though he had been stirred by Byron, later by Wordsworth,
and even by Keats,[78] he had been first apprenticed to the neoclas-
sicists.[79] Perhaps his very hostility to these implies that they had
left their mark on him; he protests too much. From them comes
also, presumably, some of his decorum. In addition, he shared
the general conviction of the epoch concerning the moral respon-
sibility of literature: that fiction, criticism, and poetry molded
character. Writing, said a critic *apropos* of Samuel Woodworth's
poetry, "exalts and purifies; or corrupts and destroys."[80] The same
critic was entirely serious when he went on to say of this popular
poet's work: "It is exactly what *American* poetry always ought to
be—patriotic, moral, chaste, and republican."[81] Bryant's phrase-
ology does not sink to this level, but his theories belong, after all,
to the early stages of American romanticism.

*   *   *

The general correlation between Bryant's theories and his prac-
tice is undeniable. "The heart," that is, the feelings, whether in
relation to a hurricane or a mosquito, animates every poem.[82] His
reference of these feelings to the "moral sentiment," as he writes
of the battlefield or of the fringed gentian, is habitual.[83] His sub-
jects are the "vicissitudes of man," whether those of Marion, "the
swamp-fox," or his own when public life deprived him of

The dear, dear witchery of song.[84]

His style is "luminous," both in its intelligibility, for which Edward
Everett praised it, and in its radiation, at least in some poems, of a
kind of spiritual light.

In his prosody Bryant continued to use the anapestic foot he had
championed in his first essay on poetic theory; and he experimented
with blank verse, rhymed iambic pentameter, the sonnet, the
Spenserian stanza, and the alexandrine. Yet he shunned novelties
in meter and language; actually he was no innovator. Indeed, in

every way the consistency between his theory and his practice is a little depressing; his reach certainly did not exceed his grasp; he set no impossible ideal for himself. As he contemplated the extravagant emphasis on reason in Pope and the extravagant emphasis on feeling in Byron, he adopted a middle course. Thus in the intervals of his busy life the journalist Bryant wrote his correct stanzas, fulfilling justly enough his announced aims. We cannot quarrel either with his sincerity or his good sense, but even these virtues hardly suffice for poetry.

For something is missing when Bryant implements his principles, something, it must be confessed, rather distressing to the reader: emotional depth is lacking; the quality of the "feelings" is thin. When Bryant speaks of "the heart" he lacks intensity. It may not be irrelevant to contrast him for a moment with Herman Melville, who, although primarily a novelist, is now attaining recognition as a poet. Different from the older writer in the boldness of his techniques and the angularity of his lines, he, too, spoke of the heart. "I stand," he said, "for the heart. To the dogs with the head!"[85] It was true; intensity of emotion pervades his poetry hardly less than *Moby-Dick*. Bryant can say:

> Let thine own eyes o'erflow;
> Let thy lips quiver with the passionate thrill.[86]

He can say such things, but about all the emotional crises in his poetry there is something a little remote, pallid, even abstract; his situations lack particularity.

Thus the heart feels melancholy among the autumn leaves, indignation at the massacre at Scio, or loneliness on the prairies, but somehow it does not matter much. The emotion appears to be somebody else's, not our own. It seems unfair to fall back upon the ancient charge of "coldness";[87] Bryant is less cold than impersonal. But all these emotional reactions lack the special stimulus, the concrete moment, the persuasive meaning. Hence the intensity of "To a Waterfowl," with its instant of religious consecration, comes as a kind of surprise, so different is it from the propriety of the "Hymn to Death," of "The West Wind," or of "A Walk at Sunset." It is impossible not to laugh at Bryant's agreeable good will toward his beloved in " 'Oh Fairest of the Rural Maids' "; in general, human passion is lacking.

Obviously a genuine correspondence exists between Bryant's theories and his practice. At the same time his stately lectures lack detail; they tell us little or nothing of subjects which deeply attracted him. For example, he writes formally of the meanings of nature to the poet, but not of his own eagerness to record American phases of nature.[88] Often, as in this particular case, these personal enthusiasms have more significance in the history of our poetry than all his pontificals on "the heart" or "the moral senti- ment." Bryant had hobbies, too, which, without developing into major interests, added a variety not always associated with his total performance as a poet. One of these was his now forgotten humanitarian poetry, his songs in behalf of Greek or Spanish lib- erty, such as "The Greek Partisan" or "The Lament of Romero."[89] Other playthings were his translations and adaptations from the Spanish religious poets. His celebration of the "storied associ- ations" of Europe was less fluent and less buttressed by learning than Longfellow's, but it was often effective, and his sensitivity to the romance of Spain extended generously to the poetry of Spanish America.[90]

There is, in fact, in Bryant's practice a half-conscious groping toward themes of increasing importance to American romantic poets, toward interests still imperfectly developed. These themes appear in little clusters of poems now eclipsed by "Thanatopsis" and by other stanzas in the standard Bryant canon. His output of verse was slight;[91] and he never gave himself unreservedly to these fresh subjects. He was a man of affairs, a busy editor; and he had announced officially what he considered to be the true prin- ciples of poetry. Yet he was sensitive to all these experiments with new subjects, such as that which so engaged Drake, namely, that of celebrating American scenery:

> Shame! that while every mountain, stream, and plain
> Hath theme for truth's proud voice or fancy's wand,
> No native bard the patriot harp hath ta'en,
> But left to minstrel of a foreign strand
> To sing the beauteous scenes of nature's loveliest land.[92]

Our landscapes Bryant loved, and there is an affinity between the panoramic scenes in his poetry and those of our early nineteenth century painters, such as Thomas Doughty, Thomas Cole, or Asher Brown Durand. In writing of Cole Bryant must have been conscious of his own aims in some of his nature poetry. He refers to an America delighted

> at the opportunity of contemplating pictures which carried the eye over scenes of wild grandeur peculiar to our country, over our aerial mountain-tops with their mighty growth of forest never touched by the axe, along the banks of streams never deformed by culture, and into the depth of skies bright with the hues of our own climate.[93]

In his poetry, besides particular flowers or trees, he had such horizons in mind, but we look in vain for them in statements concerning this provocative union of literature and painting or concerning his pleasure in our history and legend as proper subjects for poetry. He shared the romantic's curiosity concerning the "noble savage" in America and, like Cooper or like Longfellow, he was curious about the red man, but here again his theories of poetry reflect no serious consideration of the primitivism of which his poem "Monument Mountain" is a timid example.

More and more we realize that Bryant's lectures on poetry and his other critical writings neglect his own special enthusiasms. Emerson praised him because "he first and he only made known to mankind our northern landscape."[94] Nevertheless, this aim is nowhere proclaimed by Bryant as one of his primary objectives. Indeed, between his sermonic utterances on nature in the lectures and his sharp, colloquial observations in letter or conversation the contrast is vivid:

> I saw [he wrote his brother] some lines by you to the skylark. Did you ever see such a bird? Let me counsel you to draw your own images, in describing Nature, from what you observe around you. ... The skylark is an English bird, and an American who has never visited Europe has no right to be in raptures about it.[95]

Likewise, the spacious invocations in the poetry to earth and sky and the generalities on nature in the lectures should not blind us to Bryant's delicate precision in writing of American birds and flowers. He was, a friend said, "a passionate botanist" of the American natural world,[96] and on this point we can hardly do better than quote the statistics:

> The trees of his poetry number thirty, and many of them—in particular the oak, the beech, the pine, the maple—are used repeatedly, the oak for instance, occurring in some twenty poems....

> The flowers of his poetry . . . are about forty-five in number, and
> his use of them indicates a faithfulness of observation that well-
> nigh exceeds Thoreau's. Three—the yellow violet, the fringed gen-
> tian, and the painted cup—are the themes of separate poems.[97]

In the end all these interests of Bryant subserve his function
as a poet of high ethical and religious feeling. The religious
attitudes in his poetry are shifting, like those in his life: Calvinistic
(without, of course, doctrine), deistic, pantheistic, Unitarian.[98] God
is a Being unfolding Himself in breeze, flower, and stream or God
is—witness Bryant's own personal experience[99]—to be approached
as a Christian, with simple faith. No proof exists that he ever
finally resolved these conflicting points of view. Yet the "moral
sentiment," the moral law, the relation of the moral impulse to
nature,—on these he always meditated, and—alas!—on these he
often preached in his poetry. He was, indeed, far from the modern
view that the poet should set down what he feels at the particular
moment of experience; instead he inclined to the contemporary
notion prevalent in America that the poet should record what he
ought to feel. Attached to the fringed gentian, the yellow violet,
or Green River is always the "lesson." The exaltation in such a
lyric as "To a Waterfowl" is sincere, for the subterranean river of
Bryant's life was religious, but the moral tag was there, and in-
trusively appended. Altogether what has sometimes been said
inaccurately of Emerson seems true of Bryant, that his romanticism
was rooted in Puritanism.

*　*　*

Bryant's romantic gospel of "the heart" was perilous for a civili-
zation in which taste still lacked rigorous standards. Soon other
poets, chief among them Longfellow and Whittier, spoke in similar
language of the feelings to an audience even less intellectual than
Bryant's. Within a short time the two Massachusetts poets had
become the popular troubadours for a poorly educated and un-
critical America. It is, indeed, hardly possible to exaggerate the
influence of Longfellow and Whittier upon our "mercantile cul-
ture," and at the same time their remoteness from the highest con-
ceptions of the function of the poet. Both were essentially simple
men; both were incapable of abstract thought; both employed the

familiar romantic materials of legend, of the past (European or American), of primitivism, of the Indian, of individualism in social reform; and both were amazingly fluent versifiers. Their vogue helped to dispel neoclassicism; they were romantic poets. Yet it need hardly be added that they lacked the passion of a Byron or a Shelley. Longfellow and Whittier domesticated American romanticism.

Little in Whittier's writing can be honored by the title of poetic theory. His essay, "The Beautiful," actually a study of "the beauty of holiness," is a Quaker meditation on virtue; and in his discussion of Robert Dinsmore the best he can hope for art is that American domestic life may be "hallowed and beautified by the sweet and graceful and tender associations of poetry."[100] Not without thoughts, perhaps, of the Concord writers, he alluded to contemporary American poetry as "more the product of over-strained intellects than the spontaneous outgushing of hearts warm with love, and strongly sympathizing with human nature as it actually exists about us."[101]

Bookish and widely read in poetry,[102] in spite of his rustic background, Whittier became on this dubious level of æsthetics a persuasive practicer of his beliefs. Who does not respond to his tales from New England's legendary past, such as "Skipper Ireson's Ride?" Or to the laughter and tears of her rural life in "The Barefoot Boy" and "Telling the Bees," or to Snow-Bound? A large proportion of his writing deals with the individual in his quest for social reform, but all his poems show the romantic impulse filtered down to this language of "the heart,"—and to little more. A final point of reference for Whittier, as for Bryant, was God. It was, he said, his conviction that every long poem should be "consecrated to the sacred interests of religion and humanity."[103]

* * *

Whittier's rather affected phrase, his allusion, that of a well-read, shrewd thinker, to his "rustic reed of song,"[104] suggests in its final word the vague theories of these two, Whittier and Longfellow: the true poet was primarily a *singer*. Especially in the latter's writing the word "song" recurs repeatedly: the "tower of song with lofty parapet"; the poet's "land of Song"; "some humbler poet

whose songs gushed from his heart"; the poet "breathed a song";
Milton's "song"; or "the gift and ministry of Song."[105] Everywhere
we turn we perceive Longfellow's reliance upon songs, legends, and

> Tales that have the rime of age,
> And chronicles of eld.[106]

Some critics have embroidered this instinctive belief, this easy
solution of a complex function, crediting Longfellow, from his
simple prose creed in *Kavanagh*, with a theory of world-poetry as
opposed to the poetry of nationalism.[107] Others have even discovered
in his thinking (a process difficult to discover at all!) a criterion of
the universal, citing the sixth scene of "Michael Angelo," in which
the artist cries:

> I see a statue,—see it as distinctly
> As if it stood before me shaped and perfect
> In attitude and action. I have only
> To hew away the stone walls that imprison
> The lovely apparition, and reveal it
> To other eyes as mine already see it.[108]

Is this a theory? It is difficult to discover in the stanzas more than
an obvious conception of an Absolute Good, that is, Longfellow's
own particular version of "the moral sentiment."[109]

Perhaps in constructing anything like a definite theory of poetry
for Longfellow (or for Whittier), we strain too far. Except for
Kavanagh he utters no oracle on these matters, and though we
might expect it from his talent for rhyme and meter, he says
nothing worth hearing concerning prosody.[110] All his allusions to
the office of poet, like those in "Michael Angelo," are cloudy, and
in the end bring us back to his simple idea that the poet was a
singer, apart from active life, singing songs of medieval Europe,
of an idealized Indian, of life in the American village. The poet
was merely the celebrator of "some simple and heartfelt lay."[111]

Probably we should not expect more. Clear and amiable lec-
turer, patient, exact, but somewhat passive scholar, he lacked in
conspicuous fashion the analytical mind. Possibly no American
investigator of his time knew more outwardly concerning Dante
and the Middle Ages, Goethe and Weimar, or Cervantes and
Spain and at the same time so little of the penetralia of such
matters. No poet-critic could be less inward or more richly

peripheral. The art of this imitative, unoriginal poet exhibits one purpose only, the same purpose so accurately described by the friend of Longfellow's idol, Washington Irving—the Spanish novelist, Fernán Caballero. Whether he wrote of Nuremberg, of the village blacksmith, or of Hiawatha Longfellow hoped "poetizar la realidad."[112]

So, while millions applauded, Longfellow sang his songs, lifting them gently above reality into a rainbow world, and shaping them with a craftsmanship adequate for readers who craved sentiment more than form and thought. With such simplicity of purpose he became the most popular poet of his age in America, and in poetry in English he remained for his generation second in vogue only to Tennyson. What we should observe is that his theory is not less important because only half-spoken; it dominated his verse with a complete consistency. In Bryant there were, as we have seen, divagations from his large principles, but from Longfellow's conviction that the poet should "poetize reality" there occurs no truancy whatever, whether he writes of rain on a summer afternoon or adapts the *Coplas* of Manrique (or translates Dante). The shower falls softly in the dust or the medieval knight fights his battles, but everywhere, as we read, we sense this poet's belief that

> It is the heart, and not the brain,
> That to the highest doth attain.[113]

Certainly, wander where we may in the spacious, pleasant garden of Longfellow's poetry, our brains are never taxed! In view of his dependence upon literature and upon other poets and in view of his natural identification with romantic poetry, it is amazing how far he is from its leaders: the supernaturalism of Coleridge, the philosophizing of Wordsworth, the ethical passion of Shelley, the sensuousness of Keats. Instead he has bequeathed to us the poetry of "reverie," to use another word which both he and Washington Irving loved. Here is grief, softened by the years, as in "Footsteps of Angels"; regret for vanished days, as in "My Lost Youth"; or peace, as in "The Day is Done." Never tension, never reality. It is astonishing, too, when so much is omitted of all those things which make romantic poetry memorable, how much remains within this placid mirror: the lyrics of village life in America; the verse narratives of her history and legends; the dramas; the

sonnets; the translations.[114] All these he gives us, with his gentle
music. Reading Longfellow is like listening in a cowrie to the far-
off echoes of the sea, that is, of life and passion. He himself un-
consciously described his own melodies:

> Such songs have power to quiet
> The restless pulse of care,
> And come like the benediction
> That follows after prayer.[115]

* * *

By no means all the American poetry of the first half of the cen-
tury was anchored in Puritanism. Even as Bryant wrote of the
"heart" and of the "luminous style" and as Longfellow practiced
his acknowledged part as the maker of "songs," another poet, dis-
dainful in his verse of "the moral sentiment," of social liberties,
of primitivism, or of legend or scenery in America, devised more
daring principles. In spite of such heterodoxies, he, too, was a
romantic. Poe's *Tamerlane and Other Poems* (1827) appeared only
six years after Bryant's first collected poems, and twelve years be-
fore Longfellow's *Voices of the Night*, in which "the singer" laid
down his first enchantments over his myrmidons. Poe was to be
different. It is tempting to ascribe his freer æsthetics to his half-
Bohemian origins and erratic career and to his remoteness from
Puritan influences. It is tempting, too, as well as dangerous, to
link the dark egocentrism in his poetry with Byron, whom he imi-
tated, or his "indefinitiveness" with Coleridge, with whose am-
bitions for poetry he sympathized.[116] Less affected than any poet
of the entire century by the struggle, conscious and unconscious,
for the use of national elements in our poetry, Poe seems at first a
Europeanized romantic poet, an inferior one in his supernatural-
ism (he read widely in the Germans); in his medievalism, so vapid
and theatrical; and an extravagant one in his moody emancipation
of the "ego."

In these ways, as well as in the provocative richness of his poetic
theory[117] and in his elaborate techniques, Poe is a major figure,
"worthy," as Henry James says of one of his characters, "of any
whatever." We are studying him with only a brief exposition of
his famous doctrines of pleasure, taste, or unity, as a pioneer,

like Halleck, Percival, Bryant, Whittier, or Longfellow, in his creation of American romantic verse. Poe died in 1849, after an unhappy life of forty years; in his own time he had remained a minor poet almost unregarded.[118] What interests us is the strikingly different quality of his romanticism: this coexistence in America with the tepid gospels of "the heart" and "the song" of his arrogant criteria (so they seemed a century ago). He adds to our literature what Swinburne called

> one pure note of original song—worth singing, and echoed from the singing of no other man; a note neither wide nor deep, but terribly true, rich, clear, and native to the singer; the short exquisite music, subtle and simple and sombre and sweet of Edgar Poe.[119]

Keeping in mind our objective, Poe's place in our general pattern, we may repeat some of his formulas and then refer them, with a bow to the intricate problems of his prosody,[120] to his practice as a poet.

Undoubtedly in Poe's emphasis upon "taste" and in his plea for an elevated "pleasure" lurks his implicit protest against the gentility and the didacticism in American poetry—shortcomings which he denounced in many an acidulous review.[121] Doubtless, too, as poets he admired freer spirits than Bryant and Longfellow.[122] He was strongly original and, despite the close parallels in his verse to Byron, Shelley, Coleridge, Moore, or Tennyson,[123] his theories took form naturally from his singular temperament. Probably he would have left us such rebellious doctrines as "the rhythmical creation of beauty" had he never read Coleridge or had he never lived in America. Although he often mentions "eternity" and although he constructs in his tales studies of the conscience,[124] in his writing the moral law seems sublimated in his principles of art. Scholars have tried to right the balance. He was not a disembodied spirit, and their investigations have demonstrated his interest in the telegraph or galvanic battery.[125] Nevertheless, after all allowances are made for these correctives, he still appears removed from "the moral sentiment" and from the hearty aims of American life. In the deeper Poe art is first, and other ways of thought are secondary. For his theories of poetry he sought an absolute of art.

No American poetic theories of the nineteenth century are more accessible than Poe's; none has proved more stimulating,—or more vulnerable to attack![126] Probably we should now ponder on these, remembering that they were first promulgated in an America attuned to Longfellow's shallow songs. Poe's basic ideas are available, primarily, in his "The Philosophy of Composition" (1846), "The Rationale of Verse" (1848), and "The Poetic Principle" (1850). From such treatises we may learn that poetry is not to aim at truth and goodness, though in these, of course, it may participate, but at something else: "Beauty," he says, "is the sole legitimate province of the poem."[127]

Sensitivity to beauty encourages the mood of melancholy. This mood is akin to music, and in the expression of beauty, as in his own composition of "The Raven," rules, Poe believes, a pervading logic. In addition, there is his notorious canon of *brevity*, not to mention the complicated corollaries of his principles in metrics. Altogether this is a strange strait-jacket into which Poe has bound the Muse. So much is omitted that it is idle to describe the sad plight under these rigorous laws of the epic, the narrative poem, or even the lyric if not dedicated to melancholy. What a narrow litany of darkness it is! We can understand the shock to our other romantics: the bewilderment of Irving; the indifference of Bryant: the distaste of Longfellow. Yet no theories prior to Whitman's are so challenging, so free from the parochialism of current American verse.

Some of Poe's phrases will probably always be associated with his own poetry: that its aim is "pleasure"; that it resides in the region of "taste"; that it is the "rhythmical creation of beauty." Yet two qualities now seem most memorable. The first is the temper of all these directives; the animating spirit is, oddly enough, that of *reason*, of a logic that leads plausibly to what Poe makes appear an inescapable conclusion. In, for example, "The Philosophy of Composition," the argument is the thing, though the reader, amused or rebellious, often refuses to accept the closely-knit sequence of ideas, or the complacent conclusions, when, for example, Poe says, "These points being settled, I next bethought me of the *nature* of my *refrain*."[128] And so on. In fact, the *air* of logic, of "analysis," which Poe infuses into his tales[129] arises from a speciousness which dominates much of the poetry. Like the murderer in "The Tell-Tale Heart," Poe takes us through the whole house in the most reasonable fashion, without exposing its inner secret.

The theories are too dogmatic, too neat, too logical: "I hold," Poe says airily, "that a long poem does not exist. I maintain that the phrase, 'a long poem,' is simply a flat contradiction in terms."[130] Or he announces that the *Iliad* "is based in an imperfect sense of Art."[131] One after another the paradoxes follow. Sometimes sincere, sometimes theatrical, he tosses off his epigrams on the nature of poetry, until we are almost deceived by their very self-assurance. This temper is not, as at first appears, derived from the eighteenth century, of which Poe knew almost nothing.[132] It is rather part of the "ratiocinative" Poe, the Poe of mathematics, of the cryptograms, the Poe of the meticulous handwriting. One cannot go all the way with those critics who believe that such precise "unity" was the goal of all his living and thinking (witness *Eureka*).[133] Yet this habit of mind, half-honest, half-disingenuous, lends to his formal literary theories a flavor different indeed from any other ever recorded in America. However weak their actual logic, Poe's concepts of poetry sound like a demonstration in geometry.

The other unique characteristic of Poe's poetic proclamations is their uncompromising divorce from the normal emotions of human beings. Bryant wrote of "the heart" and of the correspondence between nature and man; Whittier of "the poetry of human life and simple nature, of the hearth and the farm-field,"[134] and Longfellow thought of himself as the bard of the people. All such ideals Poe either condemned or renounced as illusions. Whatever relation poetry has to such commonplaces is, he declares, "collateral."[135] After a discussion of contemporary poets who, in varying degrees, had inspired his interest, he comes at last to his definition:

> I have [he says] endeavored to convey to you my conception of the Poetic Principle. It has been my purpose to suggest that, while this Principle itself is, strictly and simply, the Human Aspiration for Supernal Beauty, the manifestation of the Principle is always found in *an elevating excitement of the Soul*, quite independent of that passion which is the intoxication of the Heart, or of that Truth which is the satisfaction of the Reason.[136]

This theory, verging on the absurd, is almost as narrow as that of the Puritan poets. Poetry becomes now not the handmaiden of religion nor of reason, but of this dim, dark goddess of "Supernal Beauty." Poe's theories were, indeed, for America, special, esoteric. Yet if these are added to those of Bryant, Whittier, and Longfellow, all of whom had watered the passion of romanticism down into sentiment, they widen appreciably our poetic criteria.

*   *   *

The relation between Poe's poetic theories and his practice has particular interest, for several reasons. First of all, his was a voice crying in the wilderness; that is, he was the first critic in America to take seriously *poésie pur*. The concepts of the other poets discussed in the present chapter are not free of compromise with the Philistine society of which they were all respected members. Poe's are. Boldly to exhort poets in the eighteen forties to search only for "Supernal Beauty" was his disturbing interjection. Second, he was, soon after 1827, though his recognition was long delayed in America, to be a poet of stature. His sharp and contentious theories, with their efficient fulfillment, won early recognition in France, where Baudelaire's "Correspondances" and Rimbaud's "Le Bateau Ivre" bore witness to his haunting influence.[137] Gautier and other Parnassians studied "The Philosophy of Composition."[138] Thus, to our chagrin, we must admit that Poe first won fame in a foreign land; and that later America reluctantly concurred. Probably the ultimate glory of his slender sheaf of poems owed something to their exegesis through his clean-cut theories, but, in any case, though Poe's poetry is limited, it remains the poetry of genius. No proof of this is needed, not even the recent tribute of William Butler Yeats, who says that Poe is "always and for all lands a great lyric poet."[139]

Unquestionably Poe's theories controlled his poetry in both content and techniques.[140] Most of his ideals for the poet have a consummation in his own verse; in his mind, as he wrote, were always his objectives of taste, pure and intense pleasure, or "the rhythmical creation of beauty." Negatively his adherence to his principles is even more measurable; his own lyrics hold no parley whatever with such aims as those of Bryant, Longfellow, or Whittier. Even in smaller, more concrete matters, he strove for consistency, for his poems are invariably brief and seldom violate, with their preposterous heroines of the euphonious names, his concept of the most poetical subject, that of "the death . . . of a beautiful woman."[141] Indeed, all the underlying depressive character of Poe the man comes out in the poetry; in it, unenlivened, as in the prose, by his sardonic humor,[142] pulsates his despair. Thus Poe's poetry, like the novels of Hawthorne, Melville, and, today, William Faulkner, re-emphasizes the mood of "The Haunted Mind,"[143] so real but so anomalous in our rather neutral American literature.

Even more definite results of Poe's theories occur in the transference into his poetry of his "ratiocination," of his "air" of reason, of his disregard of everyday life. Likewise, his analytical habits of mind compel the precision of his metrics, as in his intricate experiments in alliteration, onomatopœia, assonance, and other devices,[144] experiments so subtle that they rival or excel those of Sidney Lanier or Swinburne. In this respect, Poe's harmony of practice with theory may be best realized by a close study of the seven or eight principles of prosody which he enunciates in "The Rationale of Verse," such as his idea that poetry is dependent on time and quantity rather than on accent or by an examination of his comments on the cæsura, on "the principle of equality," or on contractions and elisions.[145] In fact, at first glance his self-discipline is terrifying; for Poe poetry seems to mean a fanatical obedience to his self-imposed laws.

Yet in this respect, not unlike some of the colonial poets, Poe could not always fulfill his own theories. The mechanical correlation in his poetry is, as said, frightening: Watts-Dunton once remarked that "Ulalume's" essential meaning could be understood without a knowledge of English,[146] so calculated were its melodies; and "The Raven," that poem, which, according to Mrs. Browning, produced a " 'fit horror,' . . . in England,"[147] is machine-made. He could not keep up this deliberate perfection. Are we mistaken in thinking that in the lovely lyric, "Eldorado," there is some emotion, some spiritual intensity not traceable precisely to those principles?

> And, as his strength
> Failed him at length,
> He met a pilgrim shadow—
> "Shadow," said he,
> "Where can it be—
> This land of Eldorado?"[148]

This poem, (unlike "The Bells"), as well as "To Helen," "Israfel," "The City in the Sea," and others, although planned craftsmanship is not lacking, reveals from the depths of Poe's nature a despair not unlike that darkening the conclusion of his tale, "The Fall of the House of Usher." The exact psychological nature of this state of mind is impossible to define though modern critics speak of it in terms of the subconscious. Nevertheless, its sincerity and intensity we cannot deny; and its transforming force makes ridiculous this "weary way-worn wanderer's" attempts to exemplify his own precepts.

For Poe, then, the emancipation of the "ego," his longing for the unknown or the ideal, or whatever we call this particular phase of romanticism, took the form of a surrender to an overwhelming melancholy. This sadness sometimes transcended all his theories of poetry. On these occasions this solemn music silenced "the jingle-man," as Emerson christened him.[149] Some poems deal with defeat, with frustration, complete and unconditional; a terrible conviction animates his denials of any meaning for life. In "Ulalume" the lover is "stopped by the door of the tomb."[150] In "Eldorado," the searcher's strength fails him.[151] The wind of death chills and kills Annabel Lee.[152] In "The Raven," even in this set piece, the answers to the lover's questions reflect negation. Will not sorrow eventually leave us? Is there not comfort in another world? Shall we not see our loved ones there? The poem is artificial, but the questions are those of a troubled spirit, and the echoing answer of them all is "Nevermore." Stronger in Poe's poetry than his icy theories is this emotion of despair.

In compensation for this sense of frustration on earth is the fierce intensity of Poe's vision of an unearthly world, real to him though it never existed, of bannered clouds, cold moons, poisonous waves, molten stars, ebon airs, solemn skies, shadowy lakes, seraphs, "shrines and palaces and towers," of

> . . . shadowy long-forgotten bowers
> Of sculptured ivy and stone flowers—
> Up many and many a marvellous shrine
> Whose wreathéd friezes intertwine
> The viol, the violet, and the vine.[153]

The details of this world are strongly visual or auditory; we see clearly the knight-errant on his horse or we hear the lutestrings of Israel. On this unearthly stage move distinctly Ligeia, Ulalume, and the Conqueror Worm, invested with some of Poe's nonsense but also, as critics have noticed, with reality. Thus Helen stands in the "brilliant window-niche," holding the agate lamp. Each particular of the imagined scene is sharply clear. This power, not vouchsafed to the other poets mentioned in this chapter, is that function of the romantic poet, exhibited notably by Poe's master, Coleridge, of making this unreal romantic world deceptively real, of giving

> . . . . to airy nothings
> A local habitation and a name.

A. E. Housman, in a remarkable tribute to Poe, has this quality in mind, but, even more, what seems at first a contradiction of this precision of detail, namely, Poe's general suggestiveness, his "indefinitiveness" of meaning.[154] This was, of course, an expression of his theory concerning "a suggestive indefinitiveness of meaning, with the view of bringing about a definitiveness of vague and therefore of spiritual *effect*."[155] We may read again in Housman's essay Coleridge's dictum concerning the pleasure poetry confers "when only generally and not perfectly understood."[156] We should then study carefully the poems already mentioned, such as "To Helen" ("The Haunted Palace" is Housman's illustration). If we do this, we shall be convinced that in his "indefinitiveness" and suggestiveness he rises above his own theories into what he called the "Supernal World," that is, a world of dark mystery and beauty. The fact is, we cannot put into words what these poems make us feel, no matter how sharp their particular details. We must let ourselves float along on the surfaces of these black seas of melody.

* * *

The foregoing conclusions concerning Poe's deviations from his official theories are themselves indefinite and undemonstrable. They are offered here merely as footnotes on his theory and practice, but they intimate one fact: by 1850 American poets had penetrated into a world of romanticism which was at least partly their own. If we think of the poetry of Bryant, Whittier, Longfellow, and Poe in its totality, it lacks, of course, unity, and, in comparison with nineteenth century English poetry, depth. Not even Poe belongs to the grand hierarchy of Shelley, Coleridge, and Wordsworth. Yet this is an interesting pattern, this of American romanticism, full of European figures (as in Longfellow's poetry) and of home-spun characters (as in Whittier's). Here may be found every phase of European romanticism, even its medievalism, but each phase is subject, as we have seen, to peculiar modification, and to changes of emphasis. In addition, here are encountered fresh elements, such as the Hudson River legend or the Indian.

By the very nature of romanticism the world of these poets is more varied than that of the poets of the Enlightenment or of Puritanism. The gulf, for instance, between such poems as "Tamerlane" and *Snow-Bound* seems wide indeed. Even these two are linked by wistfulness for the past; neither could have appeared in the preceding centuries. Perhaps, after all, the true unity of these early poets must be found in their implicit acceptance of the concept of the emancipated "ego." In this regard, they went far, but not far enough. At this moment in our story, other romantic poets were already experimenting with weightier ideas and bolder mediums of communication. After the poets of early romanticism we may turn naturally to the first verse and philosophic thought of Emerson and his Concord contemporaries.

CHAPTER IV

THE POET OF PHILOSOPHIC THOUGHT

P OE'S DISTINCTION among the poets discussed in the last chapter depends upon "The Raven" or "Israfel," but also upon "The Philosophy of Composition," that is, upon the fact that he assailed aggressively that age-old riddle, the nature of poetry. The only other American poets in the romantic tradition, whether pioneers or imitators of European models (Longfellow, Whittier, Holmes, or Lowell), to venture far on this perilous ground, were the so-called New England transcendentalists, namely, Emerson and his friends.[1] All the high moral mystery with which they enshrouded poetry seems epitomized in Emerson's haunting, inscrutable verses, "The Sphinx." In this prolonged metaphor Emerson explored the ancient problem: What is the function of the poet? These Concord men may be regarded, of course, if tested by the definitions of the preceding chapter, as romantics, too.[2] Yet so special was their adaptation of the individual's "emancipation," that we may call them, if only for convenience, poets of philosophic thought.

In their rebellion against all manner of tradition and in their revaluation of God and man, these poets invoked, naturally enough, fresh forms of expression, and so inevitably reappraised the art of poetry. Although linked to the Cambridge poets and even to the alien Poe by moods common to their epoch, these transcendentalists or philosopher-poets were original in both theory and practice, chiefly through criteria drawn from metaphysics and religion. As we look back historically, these dreamers seem far outside the accustomed patterns. Were they on a bypath or on the main highway of American poetry? On both, perhaps. There will never again be such a poem as Emerson's "Initial, Dæmonic, and Celestial Love,"—a fact we may bear with fortitude. Yet in his imagery, his bold rhythms, his structural license, and his freedoms of subject (at least in theory), Emerson cleared the way for Walt Whitman and Emily Dickinson (both of whom were aware of his craftsmanship), and even for the iconoclasts of the twentieth century. Again we breathe a different air; again we move in a changed world of poetry. With surprise we bump along over the corduroy lines of "Fable" or "Hamatreya," and with some bewilderment we linger over Emerson's 'cryptic definitions: "Poetry," says this theorist, "was all written before time was."[3]

The seventeenth century ancestors of these Concord poets had been theologians, and philosophers of a sort; it was, perhaps, predestined that this later generation, with its incalculably wider horizons, should be "Disciples of the Newness."[4] In the hard shell of Calvinism had lain hidden fertile seeds, among them the beliefs that man was essentially good and that he could know God directly. The almost comic irrelevance of this antique theology of Calvin to prosperous, democratic America; the growth of Unitarianism; the influence of German idealism, directly or through Coleridge and Carlyle; the vogue of Oriental thought; these were a few of the factors which created between 1830 and 1860 a mood as crystallized as those of Puritanism or of the Enlightenment, centuries earlier. Transcendentalism in New England was to have its philosophers, its social reformers, and also its poets. For in this stir of thought and feeling, which produced both wise men and cranks, "expression" was everything. "Expression," Emerson confided to his Journal, "is all we want: not knowledge, but vent."[5] And, less spectacular than the speech, the essay, or the novel, poetry proved to be for these transcendentalists a "vent," with some possibilities of immortality for themselves and for their ideology. In any case, their poetic "expression" remains a picturesque record of their dreams for mankind a century ago.[6]

The explanation of the universe—for it was hardly less than this— associated with New England transcendentalism is reasonably definable, more so, really, than Puritanism, the Enlightenment, or Romanticism, of which last it is a kind of sanctified corner. On the one hand, it represented more than the nebulous temper of individualism, rebellion, and reform, which its enemies, especially those outside New England, laughed at as transcendental.[7] The *Dial*, Brook Farm, Margaret Fuller and feminism, Bronson Alcott (the "potato Don Quixote") and his Concord School of

Philosophy, Thoreau ringing the bell in the church for John Brown, Millerites, vegetarians, or fabulous eccentrics,—all called forth this inexact use of an adjective applied by the German metaphysicians to a high philosophic process. On the other hand, the term as used in Concord was somewhat less than Kantian. Not many of these New Englanders breathed at the altitudes suggested by Coleridge's noble passage:

> As the elder Romans distinguished their northern provinces into Cis-Alpine and Trans-Alpine, so may we divide all the objects of human knowledge into those on this side, and those on the other side of the spontaneous consciousness; citra et trans conscientiam communem. The latter is exclusively the domain of PURE philosophy. . . . The first range of hills, that encircles the scanty vale of human life, is the horizon for the majority of its inhabitants. . . . To the multitude below these vapors appear, now as the dark haunts of terrific agents. . . . But in all ages there have been a few, who measuring and sounding the rivers of the vale at the feet of their furthest inaccessible falls have learned, that the sources must be far higher and far inward; a few, who even in the level streams have detected elements, which neither the vale itself or the surrounding mountains contained or could supply.[8]

The correlations of New England transcendentalism with Coleridge, with Kant, with Fichte, and with Platonism and Neoplatonism demonstrate the movement's hard philosophical core. Yet often the metaphysics shrank (or expanded) into mere moral aspiration. Emerson called these transcendental ideas "the very oldest of thoughts cast into the mould of these new times."[9] His analysis was elaborate, but its essence occurs in the phrases "What is popularly called Transcendentalism among us, is Idealism; Idealism as it appears in 1842."[10] He said this six years after the appearance of *Nature*;[11] through this rhapsody of affirmation and through the more concrete "American Scholar" and "Divinity School Address" his leadership had now become both solidifying and inspiring.

To be sure, the *"new views,"*[12] as Emerson called them in his essay, were almost as multiple as their believers. No two opinions were identical. Nevertheless, the subsoil of these religious, philosophical, humanitarian, or literary aberrations was this "Idealism," sometimes in its stern, metaphysical sense, sometimes diluted, as by the Reverend George Ripley, on occasion, into Sunday School sentiments. Everywhere inwardness was the goal; everywhere intuition reigned. Everywhere among these people, who were all, as Henry James said, "excellently good,"[13] was intense sensitivity to a spiritual world which could be apprehended by each soul. Naturally, in this communion the orthodox roads were sometimes avoided; many agreed with Emerson that it profaned this sacred relationship[14] to use the intermediaries of church and priest: "Let me admonish you, first of all," he had said, "to go alone."[15]

More transient, more local, and more esoteric than the intellectual patterns which have engaged us in the other chapters, transcendentalism became, notwithstanding, a dynamic movement, related to Puritanism both as a progeny and as a protest.[16] In its wistfulness toward nature, in its longing for the remote, in its emphasis upon the individual, as well as in many other ways, it resembled a species of religious romanticism. Its strength lay in its dauntless belief in the reality of the spiritual world even if this world was revealed differently to an Emerson or to an Orestes Brownson (who turned Catholic). "The three main interests of the leading transcendentalists," says a recent critic, "were philosophy, applied religion, and effective 'expression.' "[17] The underlying unity resided less in this "circle" of thinkers and writers, less in the "Transcendental Club," in the *Dial*, in social experiments, or even in the leadership of Emerson than in this widespread, pragmatic belief concerning a knowledgable, spiritual universe. Like a later poetess, who owed much to them, these transcendentalists were, in regard to their own kind of heaven, as certain

. . . . of the spot
As if the chart were given.[18]

"We are all a little wild here . . .," Emerson wrote Carlyle. "I am gently mad myself."[19]

The "madness" achieved its "vent" in many ways: in Theodore Parker's sermons; in Alcott's "Orphic Sayings"; in Thoreau's social anarchy; or in Emerson's essays. In addition, there was also the challenging, if sometimes obscure, "expression" of transcendentalism in poetry. In this medium Jones Very, William Ellery Channing, Margaret Fuller, Thoreau, and Emerson testified without too much reticence concerning their communion with the unseen. To read at length in this corporate body of poetry is to be astonished at its distilled passion. If we find in it a lack of warmth and also a touch of naïveté, we cannot help responding also to the ecstasies, reminiscent of the mystics, which animate these New England philosophic poets. Since their day the world has changed and so has poetry, but for the moment we share their exultation as they strive to

> Nail the wild star to its track
> On the half-climbed zodiac.[20]

*   *   *

Singleness of aim united the poetic theories of this ardent little band, so unseduced by the relatively worldly purposes of a Longfellow or a Poe. Since the poetry was already written in the Heavenly Mind,[21] the transcendental poet was hardly more than a celestial amanuensis. God had composed each stanza. In silence, in passivity, in humility, or in joy, as in the trance-like contemplations of Bronson Alcott or Jones Very, the consecrated poet might hear "whispers" concerning the "glorious gods."[22] Emerson had described the literary experience in the familiar lines:

> The passive Master lent his hand
> To the vast soul that o'er him planned.[23]

The concept is curiously suggestive, minus doctrine, of the Puritan's notion of poetry as the handmaiden of religion,[24] or, even more, of the ancient vates or seer.[25] In fact, a formidable moral fervor breathes through all this transcendental poetry; little trifling here with worldly moods! In the hard-headed Thoreau, this "inspiration," which the transcendentalists prized above all else, was fused with a mysterious intimacy with "life" (equally difficult to define). In similar fashion Margaret Fuller bathed in an "immortal" ocean but strove also to share the experiences of humanity. Thus there were differences, but basically the "inspiration" of the poet resembled the exaltation of the mystic. The "moment" was all; if it could be reported, form and language followed inevitably.[26]

These minor transcendentalist poets could wade but not swim in Margaret Fuller's "immortal" sea. This is to say that they are nearly forgotten; the present interest in them depends upon their occasionally vivid illustration of transcendental theories of verse. Their poetry itself is, for the most part, as unsubstantial as Thoreau's own "Smoke," with its "departing dream, and shadowy form."[27] We shall be wise in hastening on to the enduring lines of Emerson. Let us pause, however, for a moment over Thoreau's theories and practice, both of which still reflect his provocative intellect. As in the case of Emerson, we could synthesize from scattered statements in his prose a theory well-comprehended in his familiar saying:

> My life hath been the poem I would have writ,
> But I could not both live and live to utter it.[28]

In contrast to the theories of Edward Taylor, Philip Freneau, Longfellow, or Poe, it is well to observe this concept common to all the transcendentalists and well-defined by Thoreau, that the poet's "song is a vital function like breathing."[29]

Thoreau was quite honest; he was too busy "living" to devote himself completely to the art of writing, which he also loved dearly. Even the recent interest in his poetry has not salvaged a truly impressive volume of his verse.[30] His power as a poet lies rather in his apothegms, so revolutionary in his own time, so trite in their present coincidence with twentieth century theories. Emerson thought Thoreau deficient in "technical skill, but he had the source of poetry in his spiritual perception."[31] Today we are inclined to agree—if we use this metaphor—that of all the transcendentalists Thoreau's life best approximated a poem.

At the same time we could wish more actual verse from his hand. Neither in him nor in Margaret Fuller nor in Channing nor in Alcott are such aspirations, even if fulfilled, substitutes for poetry itself. These enthusiasts were wrong; art, too, as Emerson reluctantly admitted,[32] exacts its tribute. It is arresting when Thoreau says that "true verses are not counted on the poet's fingers, but on his heartstrings,"[33] but this theory of the poetic experience of the individual leaves out the reader and also the rest of the world. Thus he remarks in "The Inward Morning":

> I've heard within my inmost soul
>   Such cheerful morning news,
> In the horizon of my mind
>   Have seen such orient hues.[34]

Obviously, this is not enough. The poet must also, through a study of the art of poetry, bring his "news" to the reader.

Likewise, no study of the encyclopedic Alcott manuscripts[35] can make the dreamy Connecticut pedlar, the Concord "philosopher," the "tedious archangel,"[36] as Emerson once called him, into an Olympian poet. For Alcott the art of poetry was almost a by-product. Among the details now accumulated concerning his reading, his versifying, and his theories of poetry, there occurs this characteristic grouping: "the poet, seer, philosopher, saint."[37] Although Alcott's early tastes in poetry were formed on classical and neoclassical models and although at various periods he read for delight the metaphysicals, we may think of him as gradually drifting away from poetry into his endless philosophical treasure hunts: "I began," he says in his Journal for 1833, "to get some insight of the transcendental nature of man."[38] Thus poetry became secondary. The entry for March 9, 1850 is also suggestive. James Russell Lowell had been reading aloud to him, not altogether to Alcott's happiness:

> I look [he says] for pure idealism in poetry, and do not, I suspect, accept any mixtures in compositions of this sort. Lowell . . . does not seem to me to be an idealist. His fancy has not freed him from the understanding and given him to unrestricted thought.[39]

Lowell was at fault, Alcott believed, in not yielding to transcendental "reason"; his poetry was not pure intuition. The Cambridge poet's verse, however, has easily outlived Alcott's. As Emerson discerned in respect to Channing, the sad fact is that the rude chronicles of "inspiration" are not always poetry.[40] Despite the hundreds of stanzas in his Journals, Alcott never became a poet, though Emerson sometimes asserted the contrary with vehemence. Probably the last sentence of this tribute to his friend reveals his true meaning: "Alcott," he says, "is a poet, the only one in this country. . . . His relation to things and to men is always poetical."[41] This is about all anyone can say; he heard, like Thoreau, so Emerson thought, the inaudible voices. A few of his "reportings" of these voices may survive, but he is more likely to be remembered for his benign life, his odd methods as a schoolmaster, or even for his renunciation of animal food in order that he might become a true philosopher.[42] His concept of the poet, like his concept of the spiritual life, underlines Emerson's. He resembles his teacher in making his poetry "moral" and "inspirational," but unlike him he would not suffer the restraints of common sense.

*   *   *

An examination of other lesser poets of philosophic thought brings us to almost the same conclusions concerning theory and practice. Margaret Fuller, who sought so earnestly to bind Emerson down to earth, to draw him into her own world of humanitarianism, must not be omitted; shrewd and scholarly Margaret was nearer than these others to the actual poetic criteria of her day.[43] Yet her uneven verse reflects the confusion in her own theories, which are scattered throughout her *Memoirs* and throughout her numerous articles in the periodicals. She was a cultivated and traveled woman, with some perspective on the provincial "madness" of Concord. In her mind developed a conflict between her sophisticated awareness of the content of European literatures and her sympathy with these rural enthusiasts. For in her heart she, too, believed that the true poet was the scribe of the divine mind. Thus in her definitions she wavered, expressing at various times her faith in both "inspiration" and in human experience. She writes, with typical ardor: "An epic, a drama, must have a fixed form in the mind of the poet from the first; and copious draughts of ambrosia quaffed in the heaven of thought, soft fanning gales and bright light from the outward world, give muscle and bloom."[44]

Unlike Alcott, for Margaret Fuller the outward world or "life" (that is, in the meaning of these dreamers, noble experience) was a strong ingredient in her poetic theory. In 1846, her survey of the progress of American literature took Emerson to task for his particular deficiency. Estimating his verse, she defined indirectly her own critical position:

> R. W. Emerson [she says], in melody, in subtle beauty of thought and expression, takes the highest rank upon this list. But his poems are mostly philosophical, which is not the truest kind of poetry. They want the simple force of nature and passion, and, while they charm the ear and interest the mind, fail to wake far-off echoes in the heart. The imagery wears a symbolical air, and serves rather as illustration, than to delight us by fresh and glowing forms of life.[45]

In breadth of culture and in vitality Margaret was superior to most of the other transcendentalists. Nevertheless, in practice she, too, loved the stratospheres. As she composed her verse, much of which is still in manuscript, she lost, like Frederic Henry Hedge,

This bounded self in boundless Mind.[46]

Her best-known poem, the "Dryad Song," with its frightening, philosophical intensities, is, after all, closer to her transcendental associates than to the European poets whom she loved to praise:

> Chance cannot touch me! Time cannot hush me!
> Fear, Hope, and Longing, at strife,
> Sink as I rise, on, on, upward forever,
> Gathering strength, gaining breath,—naught can sever
> Me from the Spirit of Life![47]

Thus toward this "higher sky,"[48] as Jones Very called it, were lifted the eyes of Thoreau, Alcott, and also those of a dozen or more other New England poets. All these accepted, if they could not define, an assumption now as firmly established among them as those, in former days, of Puritanism and the Enlightenment: they believed in the law of poetic "inspiration." Their comments, like Margaret Fuller's, are dispersed, casual; only Emerson attained in a few essays a genuine synthesis of theory.[49] It is plainly impossible to disentangle here all the subtly differing strands of essentially the same theory uniting these believers in a new heavenly city of poetry. Yet we shall, I think, understand the high priest better after having listened for a moment to these acolytes of transcendentalism. On each of their altars flared up occasionally a vivid flame. Some were "single-poem" men whose verse refracted and enriched the splendor of Emerson's.

The transcendental poems were, as Emerson said in another connection, "blossoms from one root."[50] Taken with his own, they formed an entity of poetry as distinctive as the pastoral or the political verse of the "Connecticut Wits." A few poems, Alcott's "Emerson," Hedge's "Questionings," Very's "The Light from Within," or Margaret Fuller's "Dryad Song," are likely to live on, not only as examples of this singular New England poetic cult, but for themselves.[51] Still others remind us of this unflagging search for the Absolute, sometimes merely by an arresting progression of ideas as in Christopher P. Cranch's "Gnosis":

> Thought is deeper than all speech,
> Feeling deeper than all thought;[52]

or in single lines touchingly suggestive of the visions of these poets, as in that of Ellery Channing:

> If my bark sink, 'tis to another sea.[53]

This allusion of Cranch's to the subjective, to intuition was written in 1840, a year before the publication of the first series of Emerson's essays, and just after Longfellow had issued his *Voices of the Night*. Of this poetry of philosophic thought, now just beginning, the Cambridge poets were to be skeptical.[54] But they had yet to reckon with the lyrics of Emerson.

*   *   *

Essentially, Emerson's life was that of a holy man; its inner aim was through "an original relation to the universe"[55] to attain an apprehension of God. No one, then, can regard him as primarily a poet, in the way in which we salute Keats in that role; and his preoccupation with moral meanings made him, as we shall see, the expounder of a biased æsthetic. He meditated on all phases of life; no province of thought escaped the music of his "impressive inner harmony."[56] Nevertheless, more than all others in his circle, with the possible exception of William Ellery Channing,[57] he considered himself a poet. In fact, he declared: "This art of poetry,— I see that here is work and beauty enough to justify a man for quitting all else and sitting down with the Muses."[58]

Indeed, for long periods he did exactly this; he sat down "with the Muses"; he loved to think of himself as dedicated to poetry.[59] This is evident from his persistent experiments in his youth with verse; his reading; his official appearance in 1834 as Phi Beta Kappa poet; his concern with translations and occasional poetry. Yet all these associations are less significant than his realization, made clear through his *Journals*, through his commonplace books, and through the poems themselves, that in this character he could lay bare the recesses of his thought. His poems are, says a scholar, "a kind of intimate reverberation" of his essays.[60] This ideal was unshadowed by selfish desires; it is doubtful that Emerson ever expected to be known as a poet either in his own time or posthumously. Yet the mere hope of writing

> Artful thunder, which conveys
> Secrets of the solar track,[61]

fascinated him. In 1840 he confessed his longings to John Sterling:

> I am naturally keenly susceptible of the pleasures of rhythm, and cannot believe but that one day—I ask not where or when—I shall

attain to the speech of this splendid dialect, so ardent is my wish; and these wishes, I suppose, are ever only the buds of power; but up to this hour I have never had a true success in such attempts.[62]

Through his "splendid dialect" the poet became, Emerson thought, a kind of unlocker of the universe; he released "ethereal tides."[63] Thus his veneration for the office made him aware of his own unworthiness; he harbored misgivings about his fitness for this imperial role, at least more doubts than of his capacities as a lecturer or essayist. For, indeed, he had hitched his poetic wagon to a star; he would not be content with less than that "uncontrollable interior impulse which is the authentic mark of a new poem, and which is unanalysable."[64] He knew that he had power, particularly over the word or image, and he was conscious of a lightning perception which quickened his prose, but he remained humble concerning the writing of poetry. Once he lamented to Lowell that his ear was defective,[65] and at another time, as he contemplated the "continuity" of a "Lycidas" or a *Midsummer Night's Dream*, he cried out: "What we want is consecutiveness. 'Tis with us a flash of light, then a long darkness, then a flash again. Ah! could we turn these fugitive sparkles into an astronomy of Copernican worlds."[66]

Gradually, as the "fugitive sparkles" increased in brilliancy and as, in a few poems, Emerson attained "consecutiveness," his confidence in himself deepened: "I would say," he cried, "give me continuity. I am tired of scraps. I do not wish to be a literary or intellectual chiffonier."[67] So more and more he wrote of the poet and his function; more and more in his own verse he celebrated the fathomless genius of the ideal poet; and more and more he measured in such terms his own usefulness, calling himself, not altogether in jest, "Merlin," "Saadi," "Osman." Thus we may listen to his theories with respect; with all his faults he was a poet. He says gently: "Once or twice I have been a poet, have been caught up on to a very high mountain. Why should I ever forego that privilege?"[68]

"Inspiration" is too faint a word to describe what these transcendentalists meant by the poetic experience. Emerson was "intoxicated";[69] he was drunk with "God's wine."[70] Or he cries:

> Bring me wine, but wine which never grew
> In the belly of the grape.[71]

106

In his exaltation, which was almost physical in its intensity, he became, as in "The Sphinx," "the yoke-fellow" of Nature,[72] or he gave men "heavenly bread."[73] We cannot repeat all of Emerson's paradoxical sayings on this communication with the unseen—for this it really was—without losing ourselves in a sea of abstractions. Emerson's re-definitions of the poet in his terse sentences are endless, in the essays, in the *Journals*, in the poetry itself.[74] These epigrams have the challenging ring of his strong, rebellious half-truths, but quoted *in extenso* to indicate his refinements upon his primary idea, they become tedious. We must be content with his essential meanings.

* * *

The essays contain definitions, sometimes opaque, and the *Journals* offer comments and even descriptions of the ineffable experience.[75] We need, however, a translation, so to speak, of these into more colloquial phrases to acquire a working synthesis of Emerson's theories.[76] In fact, the apprentice in Emerson's æsthetic can hardly do better than study carefully two passages in his meditative, rhapsodical *Nature* (1836).[77] Although this monograph was published eight years before the more explicit study, "The Poet," and eleven before his own first volume of verse, his underlying principles of poetry, still unelaborated, were already deeply rooted in his thinking. In all essentials these principles remained unaltered at the close of his life; the valedictory poem, "Terminus," reveals him as obeying, presumably in poetry, too, "the voice at eve obeyed at prime."[78]

For besides these striking metaphors of drunkenness, Emerson employs repeatedly those of sound. The true poet can overhear— perhaps Emerson adopts unconsciously the "still, small voice" of Puritan thought—the "whispers" concerning the gods.[79] In "The Sphinx" he speaks of a "thousand voices"; in "My Garden" he hears "wandering voices in the air"; and in "The Poet" he listens to the converse of the gods, to their "dialogue divine."[80] Amid such sounds Emerson is forever distinguishing between false and true music, between the sounds of the busy world and the deeper harmonies communicated only to the poet. Thus in "Merlin" he introduces his discussion of the grandeur of this music with a renunciation of less noble melodies:

> Thy trivial harp will never please
> Or fill my craving ear.[81]

Among the other metaphors, besides those of "intoxication," of sound, of water, of food, and, of course, of "light,"[82] all introduced to describe the indescribable, is that of "flow," or "influx," which, as suggested a moment ago, may well be a beginning for our study of the poetic experience through the famous passage in *Nature*.[83] Here, without any special reasons for happiness, the mortal feels the "currents of the Universal Being" circulate through his soul, rendering him "glad to the brink of fear."[84] The experience suggests the ecstasy of Plotinus, whose influence was strong throughout Emerson's early writings,[85] and also the mysticism of the Puritan divines, from whom, in more than one way, Emerson was descended. Thus the origins of the experience in Emerson's mind are complex, but the "intuition" itself is fixed; he is certain of the divine. This union with God he sometimes described, as said, in terms of light; he spoke, for instance, of the "inlet of that highei illumination"[86] which shed its radiance upon the whole man in his relation to God. Equally bathed in light, equally sharing the universal currents, were the various incarnations, the "delegated" portions of the Universal Man: the Scholar; the Philosopher; and, also, the Poet.[87]

In one sense, Emerson hardly admits the difference of the poet from these other human manifestations of the divine: he declares that poetry includes all living beings and that the best poetry deals "not with syllables but with men."[88] Yet simultaneously he thinks of the poet as performing his unique function, that is, as relating his own particular story of the universal currents or of "the inlet of that higher illumination."[89] The poet

> Seeks how he may fitly tell
> The heart-o'erlading miracle.[90]

He is the sacred recorder. Indeed, in this regard he is, perhaps, the highest of the various spiritual fragments into which Emerson nominally divides man. Since he is at the very center of the universe and understands the relation of the finite to the infinite, he stands "among partial men for the complete man."[91]

This is a cryptic, tantalizing definition, and it tempts us to counter with all the lacks in the Emersonian concept of the poet, such as human relationships or the interpretation of beauty for its own sake. A British critic's judgment is over-mild, that Emerson's poetry was "too little clad with the vesture of human associations."[92] He is, indeed, bleak, rarefied, this Emersonian poet. Yet we must understand his notion of "inspiration," that it is an "influx" of the Divine Mind into our minds.[93] The task of the poet is to set down in finite words this tale of his collision with the infinite.

* * *

As we read on in "The Poet," comparable in its own odd way to some of the "prefaces" written by nineteenth century English and American poets, we become more and more sensible of philosophers looking over Emerson's shoulder at his intellectualized definition of the poet's "inspiration,"—and with approval. Indeed, as we read, we might say, quoting a very different poet:

> Old faces glimmer'd thro' the doors,
> Old footsteps trod the upper floors.

Plato, Plotinus, Kant, Berkeley, Coleridge, and even the thinkers of the Orient he has explored for what he calls "lustres," or for the "confirmation" of his unshakeable conviction, that "intoxication," "illumination," or "influx" are parts of man's birthright from God.

This mystical experience is the most important heritage of the poet. "For," Emerson reiterates, "we do not speak now of men of poetical talents, or of industry and skill in metre, but of the true poet."[94] Yes, "reason" in the philosophic sense, intuition, an ecstatic sense of being, a revelation of truth, like a flash of lightning illumining the heavens, an apocalypse under which "language sinks"[95]—something like these approximate the poet's experience as Emerson conceives of it. Concretely, of any particular poetic "reporting," he says: "The poem is made up of lines each of which filled the sky of the poet in its turn."[96] To write such a poem was at once the unattainable and the only worthy ideal. "I look in vain," he admits, "for the poet whom I describe."[97]

After the poet enters

> . . . . the pure realm,
> Over sun and star,[98]

—what next? How can the experience be manifested? Only one answer is possible: through nature. Turning to the passage already mentioned in *Nature*,[99] and omitting for an instant the reference to "words," we find the circumscribing pronouncement: "Nature is the symbol of spirit."[100] Sometimes Nature seems to be the "great apparition,"[101] not in the physical sense real at all; sometimes, on the other hand, she is simple reality: "the meal in the firkin; the milk in the pan."[102] Thus in the concrete and in the abstract Nature embodies the whole cycle of human experience.[103]

Both these the poet must describe, but to reveal the complete relationship, the full cycle, whatever he says must be in the radiance of his "inspiration." The whole stunning diapason, the vast "sky" that fills him, the divine "voices," these he transcribes, sometimes eloquently, sometimes haltingly, but always in terms of the natural world:

> He felt the flame, the fanning wings,
> Nor offered words till they were things.[104]

The poet in search of the Absolute, of the Good, must communicate his intuition of this through his

> . . . pictures of time;
> They fade in the light of
> Their meaning sublime.[105]

Let us understand this: the "meaning sublime" is the goal of the Emersonian poet; he attempts to communicate this meaning by these endless "pictures of time," by representations of

> Sea, earth, air, sound, silence,
> Plant, quadruped, bird,
> By one music enchanted,
> One deity stirred.[106]

For no one realized better than Emerson the vitality of even the humblest fact. Thus even in his theories he tends to center on the concrete in nature:

> The poet [he says] like the electric rod, must reach from a point nearer the sky than all surrounding objects, down to the earth, and into the dark wet soil, or, neither is of use. The poet must not only converse with pure thought, but he must demonstrate it almost to the senses. His words must be pictures, his verses must be spheres and cubes, to be seen and smelled and handled.[107]

Though Emerson uses the word "nature" with bewildering changes of meaning, he is always careful in practice and usually in theory, to seize upon a particular leaf or creature. To comprehend the "All" he focuses on the "Each."[108] The poet must never be vague or aloof; if he cannot speak of the "sensuous fact," he had better remain mute. Thus for the Emersonian poet nature is not, as in Bryant, material for a "moral sentiment" nor, as in Poe, a "backdrop," but the very essence of experience, through which he may arrive at the divine.

The poet, however, by this interpretation of nature is not only able to "leap and pierce into the deeps of infinite time,"[109] but also to give his reader a new franchise. The poet instructs him in his participation in the divine. Hence Emerson's talk of the poet as a liberator. The basic theme of *Nature* is man's alienation from God, his imprisonment, his obtuseness concerning his spiritual destiny. In "The Sphinx" we hear of man's disgrace; man is, in fact, in contrast to the serene animals, a dismal character indeed, crouching, blushing, absconding, stealing,[110] until, at last, the poet shows him the true significance of his existence. Emerson's definition of "art," (including poetry), so like Poe's in phraseology and so different in meaning, is "the creation of Beauty."[111] In fine, the poet's "art," in this highly religious and ethical conception, is to demonstrate to man the beauty of his lot; to show him that he can escape "the trammels of the Apparent."[112] The poet reveals to man what he himself has discovered with such joy, namely, that he "has pierced the shows and come out on the wonder which envelopes all."[113]

* * *

Even if Emerson was wise in adding so many cubits to the stature of the poet, difficulties at once arose. One of these is evident in his own vacillation. With his earthy common sense, he realized well enough that no poet could dwell forever on these moral pinnacles. Although he strove to hold to the belief that the best poetry is the inevitable result of communication with the divine, he could not dismiss entirely the possibility that conscious art may sometimes mold these interpretations of the unknown.[114] Certainly the conflict to which he refers, between the "spontaneous" and the "wilful,"[115] is evident in his own poetic practice. A second difficulty is related to the problem of communication. Even if the poet hears distinctly these "whispers" concerning the gods, how, in what language, shall he convey these meanings to us, particularly to the unpoetic? Language is weak; it can record for the poet only a corner of his "sky." Shall he put down these fragments, these disjunct perceptions or images? Emerson had no doubt of the answer. These children of intuition are thoughts, and thoughts in such poetry are everything: "The poet," he says, "has a new thought; he has a whole new experience to unfold; he will tell us how it was with him, and all men will be the richer in his fortune."[116]

"He will tell us,"—this is the all-important matter. Not without impatience, perhaps, at the austerities of Emerson's theory, we observe in it the relative unimportance of form: "The thought and the form," he says, "are equal in the order of time, but in the order of genesis the thought is prior to the form."[117] Though with far different connotations, Emerson's theory parallels in some ways Matthew Arnold's that "The idea is the fact,"[118] that form is a natural outgrowth of an idea. Something will be said presently concerning Emerson's idiosyncrasies in respect to language and meters. At the moment note again his continued emphasis on thought, on argument, to be born if possible of the divine, but, in any case, an insistence on thought: "For," he declares, "it is not metres, but a metre-making argument that makes a poem,—a thought so passionate and alive that like the spirit of a plant or an animal it has an architecture of its own."[119]

From this conception flows naturally the true poet's disdain, well-known to all students of Emerson, of such filagree men as Tennyson or Poe or for all verse connected with the "music-box"[120] of poetry or with the "jingling serenader's art."[121] This attitude is not attributable wholly to Emerson's Puritan temper, to his heterodoxy in matters of style, or to his allegedly defective ear, but to his principle, already discussed, that poets must be "children of music" and not merely "men of talents who sing."[122] It is foolish to play tricks on an instrument which by its very nature is imperfect:

> What baulks all language is, the broad, radiating, immensely distributive action of Nature or spirit. If it were linear, if it were successive, step by step, jet after jet, like our small human agency, we could follow it with language; but it mocks us.[123]

Can the poet describe a rainbow and all that it illumines in a sequence of paragraphs? Of course, in the afterglow of experience he may write more consciously, but since, in general, primary thoughts were "all written before time was,"[124] and since language is feeble, how shall the poet record, except intermittently, his ecstasy? How shall he communicate these "angelic radiations?"[125]

Theoretically, then, the poet has no worries concerning form and language. Before the bayonet of his ecstasy the palpable, living sentences flee out of chaos! He merely tells us how things are with him; what he hears in the secret center of the universe:

> Out from the heart of nature rolled
> The burdens of the Bible old;
> The litanies of nations came,
> Like the volcano's tongue of flame,
> Up from the burning core below.[126]

For such utterances the self-conscious techniques of the metrist were superfluous,—theoretically:

> The kingly bard
> Must smite the chords rudely and hard,
> As with hammer or with mace.[127]

Theoretically, always. Actually, Emerson admitted the need of art.

> As to the *Miracle*, too, of Poetry [he says rather sadly]. There is truly but one miracle, the perpetual fact of Being and Becoming, the ceaseless saliency, the transit from the Vast to the particular, which miracle, one and the same, has for its most universal name the word *God*. . . . But all the particulars of the poet's merit, his sweetest rhythms, the subtlest thoughts, the richest images, if you could pass into his consciousness, . . . would class themselves in the common chemistry of thought, and obey the laws of the cheapest mental combinations.[128]

Such were the hardships of the poet of philosophic thought when working in human "Time!" On the other hand, if he worked out of this time, in tune with the "heart of nature," the poem became something organic instead of mechanical, something as much a product of nature as a tree or an animal or a child. In the *Journals* Emerson distinguishes between such "organic" and "mechanical" processes, between

> the carpenter who makes a box, and the mother who bears a child. The box was all in the carpenter; but the child was not all in the parents. They knew no more of the child's formation than they

did of their own. They were merely channels through which the child's nature flowed from quite another and eternal power, and the child is as much a wonder to them as to any.[129]

It might be said that there are organic poems and that there are "carpenter's" poems. For the former the process described in "Language," in the essay *Nature*, is usual: "words are signs of natural facts," and so on. Yet in the "carpenter's" poems, too, the poet may still delight in words which are "vascular," which "bleed,"[130] which are simple and strong. Even when not under the spell of "inspiration," the poet may use such language just as Emerson under certain conditions forgave the obscene word[131] and even loved "a rattling oath."[132] Whether or not the poem comes from the "burning core" of nature, it may still repudiate the "jingling serenader's art."[133]

"Organic" poems are by their very nature symbolic. As Emerson says, the transcendental poet is committed to "this universality of the symbolic language,"[134] sometimes in words so living as to be almost the experience itself, and sometimes in the protracted metaphor of such poems as "The Sphinx." Thus metaphor, fable, myth are the natural, god-inspired idiom of the poet. The world whose materials he employs is emblematic of another:

> We are [says Emerson] symbols and inhabit symbols; workmen, work, and tools, words and things, birth and death, all are emblems; but we sympathize with the symbols, and being infatuated with the economical uses of things, we do not know that they are thoughts. The poet, by an ulterior intellectual perception, gives them a power which makes their old use forgotten, and puts eyes and a tongue into every dumb and inanimate object.[135]

Emerson was Emerson, and the roots of his theories of poetry lay deep in his own ancestry and personality.[136] At the same time his intimacies with other poets were numerous. He was far from being imitative, but his assiduous quest for "confirmation"[137] embraced reading in philosophy (particularly in his early years in the Platonists and Neoplatonists), in the seventeenth century poets, in contemporary poetry, such as Wordsworth's, and in the theory of Coleridge, whose poetry itself, in contrast to its impact upon Poe,[138] did not much impress him. As early as 1826 he had discovered as he read Wordsworth that "now and then

comes from him a flash of divine light . . . [which] makes you un-
easy that he should be such an earthen vessel."[139]

In his reading of poetry Emerson was perpetually in search of
this "flash of divine light," and also of the psychological processes
behind it. By this is meant that his respect—it can hardly be called
devotion—for the English poets depended primarily upon their
imagination, in the highest sense of the word. The explorations
of Emerson's literary debts through the years show his ascending
pleasure in Wordsworth's "idealism"[140] and his increasing interest
in Coleridge's definitions of the functions of the imagination. In
Emerson's later theorizing, in, for example, the speech, "Genius,"
or in the essays, "Intellect" or "Poetry and the Imagination,"
Coleridge's ideas are strongly present. The New Englander's dis-
tinction between fancy and the imagination is akin to the English-
man's more famous exposition.[141] Such parallels are suggestive, but
we look in vain for subservience, for more than "confirmation."
These poets merely reassured him in his own convictions.

*   *   *

Emerson was, indeed, original; his theory had its own peculiar
wildness, as if he were determined in this matter of poetry to obey
his own injunction to "write on the lintels of the door-post,
Whim."[142] Part of this seeming inconsistency arose from the
impossibility, already discussed,[143] of fulfilling his own inexorable
rules. He heard the "voices," urging him, he says, to

> Speak what I cannot declare,
> Yet cannot all withhold.[144]

Therefore he had to speak; but he could not bring himself to re-
nounce altogether the conscious processes of writing, the necessary
techniques of poetry.

Related to his symbolism, therefore, though he never anxiously
gave them names, were the devices so familiar today: the para-
doxes, the verbal ingenuities, the packed lines, the deliberate con-
trast of the erudite and the colloquial or of the abstract and the
concrete. He did not scheme about such matters too much, but
he had a general purpose in the sense that he was interested in
"prosody" as something more general than "metres." Emerson's

"plan" has already been suggested in his insistence upon the *word* and upon the *symbol*. His emphasis on these in both the "organic" and the "mechanical" processes, created inevitably a very special kind of verse.

In practice, then, in Emerson's poetry there recurred a dichotomy, either within a particular poem, or between poetry which was recorded directly from the "sky" and poetry which was in debt, in Emerson's phrase, to "the Birmingham part."[145] Thus he writes in "inspired" vein of

Bread, kingdoms, stars, and sky that holds them all,[146]

or with a planned technique which questions in this fashion: "Who will deny that the merely conventional part of the performance contributes much to its effect?"[147] A by-product of this schism, of this divided purpose, is tension, a sense of strain as Emerson strives to approach his ideal, in, for example, certain stanzas of "The Sphinx." He had overheard the "voices,"—truths concerning man, the poet, and the great "earth-mother." Portions of the revelation he perpetuated in exceptional lines, possibly in those on the transformation of the sphinx, but in the poem the vision is uneven. At other times when language faints under the strain, Emerson trails off, as in "Uriel," into philosophic argument. Instead of the "sky" inspiring each line, there is in this poem, or, to cite another example, in "Initial, Dæmonic, and Celestial Love," an imperfect dialectic.

Perhaps it would be simpler to say merely that Emerson's theories of the "sky," of the "organic," and of the inadequacy of language create obscurity in lines, in phrases, and even in entire poems. Precise meanings are, for example, elusive in "The Sphinx," and "Brahma," or even in "The Rhodora" and "The Humble-Bee." Or it might be fairer, in recognizing the discrepancy between his medium and his raptures, to point out that Emerson was, to use his own somewhat absurd word, a poet of "sparkles."[148] He was enamored of a kind of poetic "atomism." Thus our pleasure in reading his verse often depends on particular stanzas or lines. In, for example, "The Problem" occur the eloquent opening, the noble passage (already quoted) on "the litanies of nations," the less effective catalogue of natural facts, and the now classic phrases on "the passive Master." The seventy-two line poem ends with the passage on "Chrysostom," which, involved and obscure, holds, nevertheless, the memorable reference to

> Taylor, the Shakspeare of divines.[149]

Emerson cannot do justice to the whole "sky," but throughout his poetry we meet with these partial memories of his visions.

The danger is that, as we add up Emerson's various compromises, we may forget the reality and intensity of his revelations, these integrations of his rapt "spirit" with the "World-soul."[150] Again and again he could sincerely say, as in another poem,

> I yielded myself to the perfect whole.[151]

And again and again, as he sat down to write, he felt it true that language contained no shades of meaning which would do justice to the ideas which came out of these divine kingdoms of the Absolute. These "sparkles," these dazzling fragments, were records of profound religious experiences, and sometimes in short poems, such as "Days," more than a fragment has survived.

The authenticity of these experiences seems to be attested by a surprising bit of evidence, namely, Emerson's inability to remember the actual composition of certain poems:

> I find [he said in 1852] one state of mind does not remember or conceive of another state. Thus I have written within a twelvemonth verses ("Days") which I do not remember the composition or correction of, and could not write the like today, and have only, for proof of their being mine, various external evidences, as the MS. in which I find them, and the circumstance that I have sent copies of them to friends.[152]

It would be daring to say there was a connection between this forgetfulness and the flat areas in the poetry; that the vision was followed by a reaction. In any case, the incident is remarkable. In only a few poems is the exaltation sustained, most readers would agree, until the very end, in, for example, "Two Rivers":

> So forth and brighter fares my stream,—
> Who drink it shall not thirst again;
> No darkness stains its equal gleam,
> And ages drop in it like rain.[153]

* * *

With this warning we must now reconsider the less inspired portions of Emerson's verse and the effects upon this of his compromises. At the same time we must not forget his visions even while we ponder on lines from which their glory has been withdrawn. Too often a reśult of his passing from "intoxication" to sobriety or of the inadequacy of language was Emerson's prolonged transcendentalizing, so to speak,—an intellectual process of interest to no one save devoted students of his thought as a whole. The only merit of this verse is its focus in rhyme or stanza upon the familiar doctrines of the essays. Thus in "Each and All" and in "Fable" appear Emerson's poetic definitions: the One and its deceptive dispersion into multiple forms; bipolarity; compensation. In "The Sphinx" we may study the interrelations of man, nature, and the poet or the apostasy of man from nature (a theme of his early writing). "Merlin" reveals his analysis of the philosophic poet; and "Initial, Dæmonic, and Celestial Love," a poem drearier than Wigglesworth's Day of Doom, his study of the ascension of forms. Perhaps it was after reading such tedious exposition that Lowell remarked of Emerson that "few men are less sensible than he of what makes a poem."[154] This statement is too strong, but we may well wish that when he could not overhear the speech of gods, he had been content with the talk of men. Even "Hamatreya," with its earthy opening, becomes, in the end, a sermon on the Conqueror Land.[155]

Emerson's compromise with the "ecstasy" (the pursuit of which he never renounced) is sometimes evident in arid argument, such as that concerning the "Past, Present, Future," the "holy essence," or "the eternal poles of tendency,"[156] and sometimes in chilly philosophic idioms and allusions. Surely the "whispers" concerning the gods were not communicated in exactly these words! For there is too much talk of "Time," of "alternation," and of "forms":[157]

> In many forms we try
> To utter God's infinity,
> But the boundless hath no form.[158]

In "The Sphinx" we hear of the ebb and flow of pain and pleasure and of the unity of "one music."[159] The poet describes Beauty as "gliding through the sea of form,"[160] and unseen, above the heads of men, hover the "Dæmons," attending each human soul.[161] Such philosophic echoes are bad enough in any poetry, but "Uriel" contains passages directly in debt to Plato, among them the well-known repercussion of the "twice-bisected line":

> 'Line in nature is not found;
> Unit and universe are round;
> In vain produced, all rays return;
> Evil will bless, and ice will burn.'[162]

Moreover, Emerson writing in his study, though he asserted that "the great Idea" "leaves the learned in the lurch,"[163] used erudition liberally in his poetry, erudition of a more general character than the purely philosophical. Far less of a scholar than some of the other transcendentalists,[164] and only moderately interested in foreign languages and literatures for their own sakes, he was sincere in relegating learning to a secondary place in man's experience. He meant it: "Books are for the scholar's idle times."[165] Yet in the familiar phrase lurked his typical hyperbole, his rebellion against bookishness, his distaste for the "meek young men . . . in libraries."[166] For in his own way he himself was learned; the *Journals* show the wealth of intellectual plunder which he had acquired from his ceaseless reading. This flowed tumultuously into his less inspired poetry, sometimes with complicated, catalogic imagery. In "Sea-Shore," to cite only one example, he writes:

> . . . . I drive my wedges home,
> And carve the coastwise mountain into caves.
> Lo! here is Rome and Nineveh and Thebes,
> Karnak and Pyramid and Giant's Stairs.[167]

Whether casual and banal or vivid and beautiful, as in some of his references to music,[168] these allusions are characteristic of Emerson the student and writer and not usually of the Emerson "intoxicated" with celestial liquor.

Thus modification of his rigorous theories of poetry is evident in his philosophic discussions, in his philosophic diction and allusions, and in his erudite references. Not forgetting his genuine consecration to

> . . . . the pure realm,
> Over sun and star,[169]

we may find other temporizings, too. One of these is his delighted borrowing of archaic words, such as "pleached"[170] from Shakespeare or "cummin"[171] from Spenser, or of ancient, poetic names for titles, such as "Mithridates," "Merlin," or "Saadi." Another is his eager revision of stanza and line; he describes his pleasure in striking "out a blunder and insert[ing] the right word just ere the press falls."[172] Such work, he admitted, was an inevitable part of the poet's task: "Let not a man," he says, "decline being an artist under any greenhorn notion of intermeddling with sacred thought."[173] Still more we recognize Emerson's concessions to the workaday poet in himself through the living presence in his verse, so to speak, of a few great masters of the art of poetry.

Milton lives again in "Uriel"; Wordsworth in "The Snow-Storm"; and George Herbert in "Grace."[174] The writers who smote the chords "rudely and hard"[175] Emerson loved even as he loved the rugged sentences of Montaigne.[176] He liked the harshness of Donne, the ingeniousness of Herbert, and the richness of Jeremy Taylor.[177] In fact, pervading much of his own poetry is a metaphysical tinge: the "wit," the startling simile, the scorn of conventional melodies. Indeed, even Emerson's uninspired verse sometimes wears an air of the primitive, the natural, not unrelated to his lofty concept of the celestial poet. On the negative side, we encounter, quite naturally, his distaste for the eighteenth century poets, such as Pope, whose verse was, he said, "fit to put round frosted cake,"[178] or even for some aspects of Shakespeare, who in his weaker moments became merely the "master of the revels."[179] Therefore, though not malleable toward "influences,"[180] he was not wholly immune to them. The poets whom he admired, however, we might have named; his preferences were consistent with his deeper aspirations for poetry.

* * *

But what of language and meter? So careful a craftsman in prose would not be incurious about poetic techniques, and in Emerson's adaptation of many of these we perceive again the half-reluctant acceptance of the implements necessary for the practical poet. In matters of language occurs also the same ambivalence; the "seer," too, must apparently use the best device which at the moment he finds available! Occasionally, as in "Days," "Each and All," or in one or two stanzas of "The Sphinx," he is indeed the "language-maker," fulfilling his own definition: "Every word was once a poem. Every new relation is a new word."[181] Yet at other times, despite their vigor, the words are rather those of the collector, who rejoices in throwing them down, like gold coins, for their sound:

> Bulkeley, Hunt, Willard, Hosmer, Meriam, Flint,
> . . . .
> Hay, corn, roots, hemp, flax, apples, wool and wood.[182]

Such lines hardly represent "the sky" or the poet's ecstasy.

So the heavenly light shines through some images, but not through others. The symbols vary in vitality; the emblems in the "Ode to Channing" are as grotesque as those in "The Sphinx" are enchanting to the imagination. We must never forget that a characteristic iconoclasm towards the "coil of rhythm and number"[183] both motivates Emerson's half-surly use of words and also determines his heresies in stanzaic forms and meters. Thus he seems deliberately to insult the sonnet form by ending in eleven lines the closely-knit "Days," with its sixth-line, central pause like that after an octet;[184] and other poems are almost burlesques of the traditional patterns. Half-rhymes, quarter-rhymes, and "slant" rhymes are frequent;[185] and some poems contain an irritating mixture of rhymed and unrhymed lines. Or, in the "Ode," he appears to strive consciously for dissonance:

> Or who, with accent bolder,
> Dare praise the freedom-loving mountaineer?
> I found by thee, O rushing Contoocook!
> And in thy valleys, Agiochook!
> The jackals of the negro-holder.
>
> The God who made New Hampshire
> Taunted the lofty land
> With little men;—
> Small bat and wren
> House in the oak.[186]

Also, in this brief comparison of Emerson's practice with his theories, we must consider for a moment his poetic holidays, that is, his easy use of standard patterns, in his *juvenilia* and afterwards in his occasional poems. The "Concord Hymn," as melodious and almost as popular as one of Longfellow's songs, makes it clear that Emerson's jagged stanzas were not an escape for an inept metrist.[187] The four quatrains flow on as softly as the historic river they commemorate. In addition, various odes, hymns, and meditations, such as "Waldeinsamkeit," remind us repeatedly of his capacity for conventional versifying had he cared to develop it. Thus on one side of his nature he himself seems to have been the poet of "talents" whom he condemned. Facility in verse he had always had, from "Grace," written in youth, to his "Ode," published in 1857,—and later:

> O tenderly the haughty day
> Fills his blue urn with fire;
> One morn is in the mighty heaven,
> And one in our desire.[188]

This is a lesser Emerson, it is true, but in any study of his poetry we must recognize his existence, side by side with the poet of philosophic thought.

This less oracular Emerson gives us pleasure, too, in his sensitive recording of outward nature,—mountain or squirrel, tempest or flower. The romantic strain, studied in the preceding chapter,[189] was within its limitations strong in him; sometimes it moves him to beautiful imagery of nature. For in describing his beloved New England countryside he seems to forget the merciless ideal which he had created for poetry, and even the familiar mechanical devices become tolerable to him (alliteration, assonance, onomatopœia). In "Two Rivers" the sibilants echo the sound of the slow-moving stream:

> Thy summer voice, Musketaquit,
> Repeats the music of the rain;
> But sweeter rivers pulsing flit
> Through thee, as thou through Concord Plain.
> . . . .
> I see the innundation sweet,
> I hear the spending of the stream.[190]

Such stanzas parallel charmingly his prose passage on "refulgent summer"[191] in the essay. Emerson's sensuous awareness of the natural world for its own sake illustrates his own saying: "The simple perception of natural forms is a delight."[192]

This simple consciousness of beauty in nature is particularly acceptable in a poet who omits, for the most part, the complex relationships of man to man and the multifarious incidents of human life. In "The Snow-Storm," strongly Wordsworthian in spirit and anticipative of Whittier's beautiful "Winter-Idyl" twenty-five years later, Emerson casts aside all Delphic mysteries and all discordant language. Instead he uses traditional techniques to communicate to us the sounds and sights and feelings accompanying the career of the storm. He lets us hear "the trumpets of the sky," announcing its beginnings. He makes us see its all-enveloping *whiteness*. Through the long syllables and spondees we sense the pausing of the wayfarers:

> The sled and traveller stopped, the courier's feet
> Delayed, all friends shut out, the housemates sit
> Around the radiant fireplace, enclosed
> In a tumultuous privacy of storm.[193]

An interval,—and the giant goes, bequeathing us the sculpture from his mighty hand. With a craftsmanship quite as precise as any "jingling serenader,"[194] Emerson makes us survey carefully the traces of the "fierce artificer." The storm has passed, only to leave

> . . . . astonished Art
> To mimic in slow structures, stone by stone,
> Built in an age, the mad wind's night-work,
> The frolic architecture of the snow.[195]

Despite all these contradictory poetic habits, which we have studied at some length, Emerson's principles conferred upon his poetry, even within its thorny areas and within its structural awkwardness, a kind of roughhewn dignity. Often without "inspiration" in any sense of the word, but always without affectation, the angular, condensed lines stand strongly before us, as if the poet had carved them out of the granite of his own New England. In many of them throbs something like the rhythms of nature:

> Their pulses beat,
> And march their feet,
> And their members are combined.[196]

It is unprofitable to analyze them more minutely on the basis of nineteenth century criteria; some of these poems or lines have a different origin, specifically, as Emerson says, from "the burning core below."[197] If they fulfill inadequately his ideal, it is because this vision carried within itself an inevitable imperfection in expression.

* * *

As we look back over this long history, simplified in the preceding pages, of poetry from Anne Bradstreet to Emerson, we may, I think, perceive in these two and a half centuries much that is weak and imitative, but also much that is strongly original. Especially we may acknowledge in the work of a few poets (Taylor, Poe, or Emerson) courageous techniques and a common realization of poetry's emblematic character. This symbolism, like that in our fiction (Hawthorne and Melville), is both indigenous and vivid. I am conscious of a desire—not shared, I fear, by my readers—to go on with this story. I should like to describe the continued development in American poetry of an authentic language and of a bold craftsmanship, from Walt Whitman and Emily Dickinson (both disciples of Emerson), on through the evening of the last century into the sharp daylight of the modern poetic world.

This poetry of our own time has emerged exultantly from the prisons described in our four chapters into freedoms of technique and subject undreamed of by these humble pioneers. Shall we discover by further studies that we have reached our particular pinnacle of Parnassus? Or must we still wait for that genius who will know, to use Emerson's words,

> With tyrannous eye . . . the value of our incomparable materials . . . [and who will see] in the barbarism and materialism of the times, another carnival of the same gods whose picture he so much admires in Homer?[198]

Whatever the answer to this question, it is possible that the record of our recent verse might be less provocative than this story, here outlined, of the beginnings of American poetry.

NOTES

Chapter I: THE POET OF PURITANISM

[1] Probably the American novelists most widely read in France, Germany and Scandinavia are Lewis, Hemingway, Wolfe, Faulkner, and Steinbeck.

[2] In 1948 Melville was just beginning to be known in Sweden and in Norway, where interest in his writings has been strengthened by Professor Sigmund Skard's studies in American civilization.

[3] E.g., Fr. Van Roy, *An Outline of American Literature* (Brussels, 1947).

[4] See *The Poetical Works of Edward Taylor*, ed. T. H. Johnson (New York [c1939]), p. 17.

[5] European criticism of American literature has generally ignored the seventeenth century.

[6] From the title-page of *The Tenth Muse Lately sprung up in America. Or Severall Poems, compiled with great variety of Wit and Learning, full of delight. Wherein especially is contained a compleat discourse and description of The Four Elements, Constitutions, Ages of Man, Seasons of the Year, Together with an Exact Epitomie of the Four Monarchies, viz. The Assyrian, Persian, Grecian, Roman. Also a Dialogue between Old England and New, concerning the late troubles. With divers other pleasant and serious Poems* (London, 1650).

[7] *A History of American Literature during the Colonial Period.* [New. Ed. Rev.] (New York [etc.] 1897). Although first published in 1878, this book is still basic for a study of the period.

[8] E.g., Perry Miller, *The New England Mind: The Seventeenth Century* (New York, 1939).

[9] See H. S. Jantz, "The First Century of New England Verse," *Proceedings of the American Antiquarian Society*, LIII (October 20, 1943), [219]–508.

[10] See *Literary History of the United States* ... (New York, 1948), "Bibliography," III, 79–82.

[11] See Austin Warren, "Edward Taylor," *Rage for Order, Essays in Criticism* (Chicago, Ill. [1948]), pp. 1–18.

[12] See W. C. Brown, "Edward Taylor: An American 'Metaphysical,' " *American Literature*, XVI (November, 1944), [186]–197.

[13] See H. S. Jantz, *op. cit.*, pp. 222–223. It is true that the weakness of criticism concerning the seventeenth century poets has hitherto lain in its failure to see outward from within the mind of the Puritan poet, and in its rigid application to this poetry of modern criteria, of which its authors never dreamed. At the same time the general verdict must, I think, remain, that no truly great poet was produced by this civilization.

[14] *The Day of Doom* . . . , ed. K. B. Murdock (New York, 1929), p. 9.

[15] *Op. cit.*, pp. 181–187.

[16] *Op. cit.*, p. 54.

[17] See S. E. Morison, *Builders of the Bay Colony* (Boston and New York, 1930), p. 320.

[18] For excerpts from the seventeenth century writers' "Literary Theory" see Perry Miller and T. H. Johnson, *The Puritans* (New York, Cincinnati [etc., c1938]), Chapter VII.

[19] See *idem*, pp. 77–78.

[20] *Ibid.*

[21] See *The Day of Doom*, *op. cit.*, p. 7.

[22] See, in the present work, p. 88.

[23] See F. O. Matthiessen, "Michael Wigglesworth, a Puritan Artist," *New England Quarterly*, I (October, 1928), 492.

[24] Commonplace Book, January 29, 1661, quoted *idem*, p. 497.

[25] *The Day of Doom*, *op. cit.*, pp. 7–8.

[26] *The Poetical Works of Edward Taylor*, *op. cit.*, p. 33.

[27] *Ibid.*

[28] See "Preface" to the *Bay Psalm Book*, quoted in *The Puritans*, *op. cit.*, p. 672.

[29] See "Preface," *The Day of Doom* ([Cambridge, 1662]), quoted in *idem*, p. 667.

[30] *Idem*, p. 686.

[31] See *idem*, pp. 570–573.

[32] *Idem*, p. 549.

[33] *Idem*, p. 666.

[34] "Merlin," *The Complete Works of Ralph Waldo Emerson*, ed. E. W. Emerson ([Boston and New York, 1903–04]), IX, [120].

[35] John Bulkley, "Preface to Wolcott's *Poetical Meditations*," *The Puritans*, *op. cit.*, p. 682.

[36] Quoted in *Handkerchiefs from Paul* . . . , ed. K. B. Murdock (Cambridge, [Massachusetts], 1927), pp. liv–lv.

[37] *Ibid.*

[38] See Austin Warren, *op. cit.*, p. 203.

[39] H. S. Jantz, *op. cit.*, p. 223.

[40] See *idem*, p. 228.

[41] *The Poetical Works of Edward Taylor*, *op. cit.*, p. 165.

[42] See R. W. Emerson, "Language," *The Complete Works of Ralph Waldo Emerson*, *op. cit.*, I, 25.

[43] See H. S. Jantz, *op. cit.*

[44] Every historian of the period emphasizes the fact that in proportion to the population of the colony *The Day of Doom* was "a best-seller." E.g., see *The Day of Doom*, *op. cit.*, p. iii.

[45] *The Puritans*, *op. cit.*, p. 663.

[46] *The Poetical Works of Edward Taylor*, *op. cit.*, p. 123.

[47] *The Puritans*, *op. cit.*, p. 556.

[48] Of these only eleven are known to be extant.

⁴⁹ *The Puritans, op. cit.*, p. 556.

⁵⁰ *Ibid.*

⁵¹ See *Handkerchiefs from Paul, op. cit.*, pp. lvi–lvii.

⁵² *Idem*, pp. 36–37.

⁵³ *Idem*, p. liv.

⁵⁴ See Benjamin Franklin, "The Dogood Papers," *The Writings of Benjamin Franklin*, ed. A. H. Smyth (New York, London, 1905–07), II, 24.

⁵⁵ *The Puritans, op. cit.*, pp. 583–585.

⁵⁶ *Idem*, p. 630.

⁵⁷ *Idem*, p. 631.

⁵⁸ See *idem*, pp. 636–640.

⁵⁹ *Idem*, pp. 641–650.

⁶⁰ For accounts of these poets, see H. S. Jantz, *op. cit., passim.*

⁶¹ R. W. Emerson, "The Humble-Bee," *The Complete Works of Ralph Waldo Emerson, op. cit.*, IX, 41.

⁶² Cotton Mather, *Magnalia Christi Americana* (Hartford, 1855,'53), I, 135.

⁶³ *The Day of Doom, op. cit.*, p. v.

⁶⁴ See *The Puritans, op. cit.*, p. 573.

⁶⁵ See "In Reference to Her Children, 23 June, 1659," *The Poems of Mrs. Anne Bradstreet*, ed. C. E. Norton ([New York] 1897), p. 275.

⁶⁶ See S. E. Morison, *Builders of the Bay Colony, op. cit.*, p. 321.

⁶⁷ *The Puritans, op. cit.*, p. 581.

⁶⁸ "The Four Seasons of the Year," *The Poems of Mrs. Anne Bradstreet, op. cit.*, p. 79.

⁶⁹ "The Author to Her Book," *idem*, p. 266.

⁷⁰ *Idem*, p. 270.

⁷¹ "Contemplations," *idem*, p. 257.

⁷² *Idem*, p. 344.

⁷³ "The Flesh and the Spirit," *idem*, p. 261.

⁷⁴ *The Day of Doom, op. cit.*, p. iii.

⁷⁵ See Cotton Mather, *A Faithful Man, Described and Rewarded. Some Observable & Serviceable Passages in the Life and Death of Mr. Michael Wigglesworth* (Boston, 1705).

⁷⁶ *The Day of Doom, op. cit.*, pp. 1–5.

⁷⁷ *Idem* p. v.

⁷⁸ *Ibid.*

⁷⁹ Diary, quoted in idem, p. v.

⁸⁰ *Idem*, p. 57.

⁸¹ Commonplace Book, quoted by F. O. Matthiessen, *op. cit.*, p. 495.

⁸² *Ibid.*

⁸³ Jonathan Mitchel, "On the Following Work, and its Author," Michael Wigglesworth, *The Day of Doom* (Boston, 1751), p. 10, quoted, *idem*, p. 492.

⁸⁴ *The Day of Doom, op. cit.*, p. 54.

⁸⁵ *Idem*, p. 64.

⁸⁶ See Austin Warren, *op. cit.*

⁸⁷ See W. C. Brown, *op. cit.*

⁸⁸ *Idem*, p. 197.

⁸⁹ Already there appears to be a reaction. For an attack on the elevation of Taylor to a higher place in poetry than he deserves, see S. E. Lind, "Edward Taylor: A Revaluation," *New England Quarterly*, XXI (December, 1948), 518–530. Yet a more recent estimate calls Taylor "incomparably the best of our colonial poets." See R. H. Pearce, "Edward Taylor: The Poet as Puritan," *idem*, XXIII (March, 1950), 31.

⁹⁰ *The Poetical Works of Edward Taylor, op. cit.*, p. 14.

⁹¹ *Idem*, p. 15.

⁹² *Ibid.*

⁹³ T. H. Johnson, "Some Edward Taylor Gleanings," *New England Quarterly*, XVI (June, 1943), 284.

⁹⁴ See W. C. Brown, *op. cit.*; T. H. Johnson, "The Topical Verses of Edward Taylor," *Publications of the Colonial Society of Massachusetts*, XXXIV (1942), 513–554; Nathalia Wright, "The Morality Tradition in the Poetry of Edward Taylor," *American Literature*, XVIII (March, 1946), [1]–17; etc., etc.

⁹⁵ *The Poetical Works of Edward Taylor, op. cit.*, p. 149.

⁹⁶ *Idem*, p. 33, 67.

⁹⁷ *Idem*, pp. 65, 99, 106, 109.

⁹⁸ *Idem*, p. 125.

⁹⁹ See W. C. Brown, *op. cit.*, p. 190.

¹⁰⁰ *The Poetical Works of Edward Taylor, op. cit.*, p. 61.

CHAPTER II: THE POET OF THE ENLIGHTENMENT

¹ See E. A. and G. L. Duyckinck, *Cyclopædia of American Literature. . .* (New York, 1855), I, 116.

² "To********* Desiring to Borrow Pope's Homer," *idem*, I, 118.

³ *Hurd's Letters on Chivalry and Romance*, ed. E. J. Morley (London, 1911), p. 154. See also James Sutherland, *A Preface to Eighteenth Century Poetry* (Oxford, 1948), pp. 1–2.

⁴ *The Writings of Benjamin Franklin*, ed. A. H. Smyth (New York, London, 1905–07), I, 240.

⁵ Thomas Hobbes, *Leviathan*, ed. A. D. Lindsay (London, New York [etc., 1928]), p. 33, quoted by James Sutherland, *op. cit.*, p. 3.

⁶ E.g., Increase and Cotton Mather. See *Selections from Cotton Mather*, ed. K. B. Murdock (New York [c1926]), pp. xix–xxii.

⁷ Merle Curti, *The Growth of American Thought*, (New York and London [c1943]), p. 107.

⁸ "Reflections on the Constitution, or Frame of Nature," *Poems of Freneau*, ed. H. H. Clark (New York [c1929]), p. 415.

⁹ See Merle Curti, *op. cit.*, pp. 106–109.

¹⁰ See *idem*, p. 87.

¹¹ "The Spacious Firmament on High," *The Miscellaneous Works of Joseph Addison*, ed. A. C. Guthkelch (London, 1914), I, 216.

[12] "On the Uniformity and Perfection of Nature," *Poems of Freneau, op. cit.*, p. 423.

[13] See C. L. Becker, *The Heavenly City of the Eighteenth-Century Philosophers* (New Haven, 1932).

[14] *Selections from the Works of Thomas Paine*, ed. A. W. Peach (New York [c1928]), p. 251.

[15] Thomas Carlyle, "The Hero as Man of Letters," *On Heroes, Hero-Worship and the Heroic in History* (London [1922]), pp. 159–160.

[16] See Merle Curti, *op. cit.*, Chap. V, "The Rise of the Enlightenment." Although these ideas are emphasized in this brief outline in order to indicate the concepts affecting American poetry, we must not forget the eighteenth century interest in emotion or sympathy or other aspects of the imagination "from the angle of simple association, that form in which the imagination was probably most generally considered in the eighteenth century." See Kenneth MacLean, "Imagination and Sympathy: Sterne and Adam Smith," *Journal of the History of Ideas*, X (June,1949), 399.

[17] Quoted by Kenneth MacLean, *England in the Eighteenth Century* (Toronto, 1942), p. 7.

[18] See, in particular, *A Poem on Industry*, *The Miscellaneous Works of David Humphreys* (New-York, 1804), pp. [89]–114.

[19] See Timothy Dwight, *Greenfield Hill: a Poem in Seven Parts* (New-York, 1794), Parts II and VI.

[20] See Joel Barlow, *The Columbiad, a Poem* (Philadelphia, 1807), p. 299.

[21] See *idem*, p. 309.

[22] *The Works of Herman Melville*, Standard Ed. (London [etc.] 1922–24), VIII, 274.

[23] The most helpful definition of relevant poetic theory occurs in the recent volume by James Sutherland, *A Preface to Eighteenth Century Poetry, op. cit.* An example of the consideration of special phases is R. K. Root, *The Poetical Career of Alexander Pope* (Princeton, London, 1938). See, in particular, Chapters I and II. See also Geoffrey Tillotson, *Essays in Criticism and Research* (Cambridge, 1942), Chaps. VII, VIII.

[24] Although this book is not primarily concerned with the problem, some of the differences in the treatment of various forms by various poets are suggested in Leon Howard, *The Connecticut Wits* (Chicago, Ill. [1943]).

[25] Trumbull's theories of poetry are often discernible in his literary criticism, of which a substantial body still remains in manuscript. For his notions concerning the epic, burlesque, satire, description, diction, etc., see Alexander Cowie, "John Trumbull as a Critic of Poetry," *New England Quarterly*, XI (December, 1938), 773–793. All of Trumbull's theories are hardly more than special adaptations of English principles to his American subjects, and are painfully consistent with the basic convictions of the age.

[26] For an account of the newspaper advertisements of such books see Alexander Cowie, *John Trumbull, Connecticut Wit* (Chapel Hill, 1936), p. 148.

[27] See, in the present chapter, p. 55.

[28] Although Agnes Marie Sibley gives an excellent survey of "the reading of Pope in America" as well as opinion about him "as a moralist," "as a rheto-

rician," and "as a poet," in her book, *Alexander Pope's Prestige in America, 1725–1835* (New York, 1949), she makes no detailed attempt to study his influence on the writers discussed in the present chapter. Dr. Eva B. Dykes has written a dissertation (Radcliffe College, 1920), entitled "Pope and His Influence in America." This thesis is chiefly concerned with "tracing phrasal echoes of Pope and imitations of his verse form in American poetry up to 1850." See A. M. Sibley, p. ix.

29 For discussion of these ideas in English poetry, see James Sutherland, *op. cit.*, pp. 2–4; 24; and *passim*.

30 See R. K. Root, *op. cit.*, pp. 12–19.

31 See Alexander Cowie, *John Trumbull, Connecticut Wit, op. cit.*, pp. 59–60.

32 For a discussion of these "American" modifications, see Alexander Cowie, "John Trumbull as a Critic of Poetry," *op. cit.*, pp. 784–790.

33 "To Mr. Pope on His Windsor-Forest," *The Works of Mr. Alexander Pope* (London, 1717), p. [20].

34 It is, however, impossible to state finally that the heroic couplet was more popular than octosyllabics and blank verse. It has been said that an important event in the history of our poetry occurred in 1699 when Doctor Benjamin Colman introduced into America the verse of Blackmore and Waller. Colman himself imitated Dryden, and Jane Turell, his daughter, copied Pope. See G. W. Allen, *American Prosody* (New York, Cincinnati [etc., c1935]), pp. 23–24.

35 See A. D. Culler, "Edward Bysshe and the Poet's Handbook," *Publications of the Modern Language Association*, LXIII (September, 1948), 858–885.

36 See H. H. Clark, "What Made Freneau the Father of American Poetry?" *Studies in Philology*, XXVI (January, 1929), 6.

37 See, in the present chapter, p. 64.

38 See Leon Howard, "Thomas Odiorne: An American Predecessor of Wordsworth," *American Literature*, X (January, 1939), [417]–436.

39 *Historical Magazine*, IV (July, 1860), 195, quoted in *idem*, p. [417].

40 See G. W. Allen, *op. cit.*, p. 24.

41 Quoted by Alexander Cowie, "John Trumbull as a Critic of Literature," *op. cit.*, p. 776.

42 See *idem*, p. 787. Trumbull's professions of liberalism in his essay on the arts found little fulfillment in practice. See Alexander Cowie, *John Trumbull, Connecticut Wit, op. cit.*, p. 62.

43 See Alexander Cowie, "John Trumbull as a Critic of Literature," *op. cit.*, p. 777.

44 Quoted in *ibid*.

45 "Wordsworth thought of the poet as a 'man speaking to men,' and clearly this is the implied view of all poets. It depends on what the poet means by 'man' and what by 'men.' If the late seventeenth and early eighteenth centuries had used this phrase, as they might well have done, they would have meant by 'man' the poet in his capacity as member of a civilized society, and by 'men' the other members of that closed society who resembled him in all but poetic gifts." Geoffrey Tillotson, *op. cit.*, p. 53.

46 See *The Complete Works of Ralph Waldo Emerson*, ed. E. W. Emerson ([Boston and New York, 1903–04]), I, 12–14.

[47] See Kenneth MacLean, *England in the Eighteenth Century, op. cit.,* p. 9.

[48] *Greenfield Hill, op. cit.,* p. 15.

[49] Kenneth MacLean, *England in the Eighteenth Century, op. cit.,* p. 11.

[50] Quoted in *Poems of Freneau, op. cit.,* p. xlviii.

[51] *A Poem on Industry, The Miscellaneous Works of David Humphreys, op. cit.,* p. 103.

[52] For a discussion of this concept in English poetry, see James Sutherland, *op. cit.,* pp. [83]–102. This view influenced strongly the poetic theory of the "Philadelphia Group." See, in the present chapter.

[53] *Greenfield Hill, op. cit.,* p. 13.

[54] See, in the present work, p. 123.

[55] Winthrop Sargent, ed., *Selections of the Loyalist Poetry of the Revolution* (Philadelphia, 1857), p. 12, quoted in M. C. Tyler, *The Literary History of the American Revolution, 1763–1783,* (New York, London, 1897), II, 125.

[56] Quoted in *Poems of Freneau, op. cit.,* p. xix.

[57] For an account of this circle, see *idem,* p. xv.

[58] *Philosophic Solitude: or, The Choice of a Rural Life. A Poem. By a Gentleman Educated at Yale College* (New-York, 1747), p. 17. See the account of Livingston in M. C. Tyler, *A History of American Literature* (New York, 1878), II, 218–220. One strong influence apparent in *Philosophic Solitude* was *The Choice,* a poem by John Pomfret.

[59] See James Sutherland, *op. cit.,* pp. 158–159.

[60] Recent criticism has given these poets more attention. See *Literary History of the United States* (New York, 1948), I, 93–100.

[61] Actually Mrs. Ferguson lived at Graeme Park, about twenty miles from Philadelphia.

[62] "A Parody on the foregoing Lines, by a Lady, assuming the Name of Laura," Nathaniel Evans, *Poems on Several Occasions* (Philadelphia, 1772), p. 149.

[63] See "To Benjamin Franklin, Esq; L. L. D.," *idem,* pp. 108–109.

[64] Quoted in E. A. and G. L. Duyckinck, *op. cit.,* I, 177.

[65] Celebrated by Joel Barlow in Book VIII of *The Columbiad.* See, in the present chapter, p. 41.

[66] See Thomas Godfrey, *Juvenile Poems on Various Subjects. With the Prince of Parthia, a Tragedy* (Philadelphia, 1765), p. xii.

[67] In various poems Godfrey echoed Dryden, Pope, Gray, Young, Shenstone, Prior, and Collins. See G. W. Allen, *op. cit.,* p. 25.

[68] See A. H. Quinn, *A History of the American Drama from the Beginning to the Civil War* (New York, 1923), p. 24.

[69] Thomas Godfrey, *op. cit.,* p. 191.

[70] *Familiar Letters of John Adams and His Wife Abigail Adams,* ed. C. F. Adams (New York, Cambridge, 1876), pp. 215–217.

[71] *The Miscellaneous Essays and Occasional Writings of Francis Hopkinson, Esq.* (Philadelphia, 1792), III, 169.

[72] *Idem,* p. 171.

[73] See Leon Howard, *op. cit.;* and V. L. Parrington, ed., *The Connecticut Wits* (New York [c1926]), "Introduction."

[74] See Alexander Cowie, *John Trumbull, Connecticut Wit, op. cit.,* pp. 97–101.

75 See V. L. Parrington, *op. cit.*, p. [154].

76 See Samuel Kettell, *Specimens of American Poetry, with Critical and Biographical Notices* (Boston, 1829), I, 176n.

77 Leon Howard, *op. cit.*, pp. 26–27.

78 *Idem*, p. 28. For a study of the theoretical relation of "taste" to "reason," see R. K. Root, *op. cit.*, pp. 12–19.

79 V. L. Parrington, *op. cit.*, p. 415.

80 *Idem*, pp. 428–514.

81 See Alexander Cowie, *John Trumbull, Connecticut Wit, op. cit.*, p. 205.

82 *The Progress of Dulness, or The Rare Adventures of Tom Brainless* (Exeter, 1794), p. 48.

83 *M'Fingal: An Epic Poem*, ed. B. J. Lossing (New York, 1881), p. 109.

84 "The Critical Reader will discern, that I have rather proposed to myself Swift & Churchill as models in my Hudibrastic writings, than the author of Hudibras." Quoted by Alexander Cowie, *John Trumbull, Connecticut Wit, op. cit.*, p. 151. Yet Butler (and Prior, too) influenced *M'Fingal*.

85 "True Wit is always accompanied with good nature, politeness, and a fine taste." "The Meddler, Number II," *Boston Chronicle*, II (September 14–18, 1769), 298.

86 "*Hudibras* Trumbull regarded as low burlesque and *M'Fingal* as high burlesque." Alexander Cowie, "John Trumbull as a Critic of Poetry," *op. cit.*, p. 783. Cf. *supra*, p. 45. Probably even this small branch of poetic theory must be regarded as part of the English tree. Its interest resides in Trumbull's explicit definition and his adaptation of it to American materials. For studies of types of burlesque poetry which doubtless shaped Trumbull's theories, see Cowie, "John Trumbull as a Critic of Poetry," p. 783.

87 Almost at once Trumbull was acclaimed as a disciple of Pope. The *Connecticut Journal* for November 30, 1770, published verses in his honor which began as follows:

> Immortal POPE! thy SON immortal see:
> He treads the steps that once were trod by thee.

Quoted by Alexander Cowie, *John Trumbull, Connecticut Wit, op. cit.*, p. 62.

88 See Leon Howard, *op. cit.*, p. 83.

89 Quoted in V. L. Parrington, *op. cit.*, p. [154].

90 This poem shows the wide use in America of English neoclassic prosody; it employs heroic couplets, blank verse, octosyllabics, and Spenserian stanzas. See G. W. Allen, *op. cit.*, p. 25. For a discussion of Dwight's meters in *Greenfield Hill*, see Leon Howard, *op. cit.*, pp. 229–230.

91 *Greenfield Hill, op. cit.*, pp. 45–46.

92 V. L. Parrington, *op. cit.*, p. 340.

93 *The Columbiad* contained long passages on Mexico and Peru.

94 Joel Barlow, *op. cit.*, p. x.

95 Humphreys's verse was indebted to the devices in John Ward's *A System of Oratory*. See Leon Howard, *op. cit.*, p. 120.

96 "A Letter to a Young Lady in Boston. Dated at New-Haven, April, 1780," *The Miscellaneous Works of David Humphreys* (New-York, 1790), p. 96.

[97] *A Poem on Industry, The Miscellaneous Works of David Humphreys* (New-York, 1804), p. 107.

[98] *The Poems of Philip Freneau*, ed. F. L. Pattee (Princeton, N. J., 1902–07), I, 34.

[99] *Idem*, I, 35.

[100] Quoted in *Poems of Freneau, op. cit.*, p. xvi.

[101] *Ibid.*

[102] "A Political Litany," *idem*, p. 21.

[103] *The Poems of Philip Freneau*, ed. F. L. Pattee, *op. cit.* II, 371.

[104] Freneau lived on until 1832, but showed no real awareness of the romantic revival. As late as 1815 he published a poem in heroic couplets, and, in general, gave no hint of his escape from the orthodox meters. Indeed, Freneau's prosody exhibits little originality. See, however, his use of the anapest in "Pictures of Columbus." G. W. Allen, *op. cit.* p. 2.

CHAPTER III: THE POET OF EARLY ROMANTICISM

[1] An amusing summary of these heterogeneous opinions concerning romanticism occurs in H. M. Jones, *Ideas in America* (Cambridge, Mass., 1944), Chapter VI.

[2] E. g., René Wellek and Austin Warren, *Theory of Literature* (New York, [1949]), pp. 276–280. This book describes in detail the confusion of terms.

[3] "Carl Becker has suggested that romanticism, with its emphasis on sentiment, was the chief means by which the sons of the Enlightenment attempted to solve the problem of evil. . . ." Merle Curti, *The Growth of American Thought* (New York and London [c1943]), p. 121.

[4] See, in the present work, p. 62.

[5] For a suggestive and detailed account of the rear guard actions of neoclassicism in America and of the gradual victory of romanticism, see *Minor Knickerbockers; Representative Selections*, ed. K. B. Taft (New York, Cincinnati [etc., 1947]), pp. lxiv–lxxii.

[6] "We mean either the temper or the expression in literature of some form of idealization, of departure from the commonplace and portrayal of the exceptional, the marvelous, the mysterious . . . . recovery of the past . . . the revolt against tradition and authority . . . humanitarian sympathy . . . individual rights; a fresh perception of nature, the renascence of wonder; and in general an ascendancy of feeling and imagination." *The Reinterpretation of American Literature*, ed. Norman Foerster (New York [c1928]), p. 120.

[7] Quoted by H. A. Beers, *A History of English Romanticism in the Nineteenth Century* (New York, 1901), p. vi. See also Ferdinand Brunetière, *Manual of the History of French Literature*, tr. R. Derechef (London, 1898), pp. 394–395.

[8] See, for example, the discussion, by G. A. Borgese, in the *Encyclopaedia of the Social Sciences* (New York, [1930–35]), XIII, 426–434.

9 Beside the traits summarized in note 6 on page 132, see the list of characteristics in "Romanticism," *Dictionary of World Literature*, ed. J. T. Shipley (New York [c1943]), p. 492–493.

10 Barrett Wendell, *A Literary History of America* (New York, 1931), p. 431. See also H. N. Fairchild, *The Romantic Quest* (New York, 1931), p. 251. See also Paul Van Tieghem, *L'Ère romantique; le romantisme dans la littérature européenne* (Paris, 1948); and René Wellek and Austin Warren, *Theory of Literature*, *op. cit.*, p. 280.

11 For evidence of the influence of English contemporary poetry, see, among other books, W. E. Leonard, *Byron and Byronism in America* (Boston, 1905); Annabel Newton, *Wordsworth in Early American Criticism* (Chicago, Ill., [1928]); H. E. Rollins, *Keats' Reputation in America to 1848* (Cambridge, Mass., 1946). Although he was read much earlier by Bryant and others, Wordsworth's influence was slight until the year 1824. See Annabel Newton, *op. cit.*, p. 189. See also J. O. Eidson, *Tennyson in America* ... (Athens, [Ga.] 1943); Julia Power, *Shelley in America in the Nineteenth century* ... ([Lincoln, 1940]).

12 In addition, the romanticism of France and Germany exerted influences hardly less potent. See in the present chapter, pp. 70, 86.

13 *Edgar Allan Poe; Representative Selections* ..., ed. Margaret Alterton and Hardin Craig (New York, Cincinnati [etc., c1935]), p. xxi.

14 We must never forget that the attitudes of romanticism (the longing for the remote, the glorification of the individual, the emotionalism, etc.) were strongly opposed on moral grounds during the first half of the nineteenth century by critics, editors, ministers of the churches, and by individual citizens in great numbers. See William Charvat, *The Origins of American Critical Thought, 1810–1835* (Philadelphia, 1936), Chap. II.

15 See Nathaniel Hawthorne, *The Marble Faun, or The Romance of Monte Beni* (Boston and New York [1888]), "Preface," p. 15; and Henry James, *Hawthorne* (New York and London, 1899), pp. 2–3.

16 "The Personal Opinions of Honoré de Balzac," *The Works of Balzac*, tr. K. P. Wormeley ([Boston, 1899–1900]), XXXIII, 118.

17 Quite apart from their inferiority in talent, all these differences may be perceived in the poetry of Halleck, Percival, Sands, Morris, Woodworth, Bryant, Longfellow, and Whittier if their work is compared with that of the English nineteenth century poets. Though less learned than Longfellow and in some respects less philosophic than Bryant, Poe was the most subtly cultivated of all these early American poets.

18 "The more restricted sense in which I have chosen to employ it, the mediævalising literature of the nineteenth century. ..." H. A. Beers, *A History of English Romanticism in the Nineteenth Century*, *op. cit.*, p. v.

19 "Poetry To-Day in America," *The Complete Writings of Walt Whitman*, Camden Ed. (New York London [1902]), V, 207.

20 *The Innocents Abroad; A Connecticut Yankee in King Arthur's Court*, etc.

21 See S. T. Williams "Cosmopolitanism in American Literature until 1880," *The American Writer and the European Tradition*, ed. Margaret Denny and W. H. Gilman (Minneapolis, 1950), pp. 45–62.

[22] American romanticism was, of course, more likely to be original, if at all, in its celebration of the western snow-capped mountains or of the Indians.

[23] These are the two characteristics which R. E. Spiller, in a stimulating essay, suggests should orient us in a study of American romanticism. Romanticism, cannot, he believes, be considered as a revolt against neoclassicism. He says (p. 345):

> Neoclassicism appeared sporadically in American literature toward the end of the eighteenth century, but it never took hold and never became a part of our indigenous literary history. The whole concept of romanticism as a revolt against neoclassicism is invalid for our literature because we had no common literary criteria, no schools, and no traditions of our own at the time when the revolt was taking place in Europe. There was no neoclassical movement as such in American literature because there were virtually no literary traditions.

See "Critical Standards in the American Romantic Movement," *College English*, VIII (April, 1947), 344–352. Yet Bryant, Halleck, and others, though they formed no coterie, specifically attacked neoclassicism. Even if American literature at this time lacked "self-consciousness," it *shared* (if a little later) the European revolt against neoclassicism, and was changed in character by the concurrent growth on both sides of the Atlantic of romantic principles. We can, therefore, designate our poets as those of neoclassicism and those of romanticism, and study them as inheritors of the two traditions, in spite of the deep roots of nationalism, more effectively in this way than as poets of "imitation" and poets of "nationalism."

[24] See his "Reflections on the Literary Delinquency of America," *North American Review*, II (November, 1815), 39, as quoted by W. E. Sedgwick, "The Materials for an American Literature," *Harvard Studies and Notes in Philology and Literature*, XVII (1935), 143.

[25] *The Marble Faun, loc. cit.*

[26] See W. E. Sedgwick, *op. cit., passim.*

[27] See *An Oration Pronounced at New-Haven, before the Society of Phi Beta Kappa, September 12, 1826, On some of the Considerations Which Should Influence an Epic or a Tragic Writer, in the Choice of an Era* (New-Haven, 1826), p. 30. Hillhouse's concern with *Hadad* was part of a wide-spread interest in Oriental themes. See William Charvat, *op. cit.*, p. 67–69. See C. T. Hazelrigg, "James Abraham Hillhouse: a Biographical Study," unpublished dissertation, Yale University, 1947.

[28] "Modern Literature," *Atlantic Magazine*, I (May, 1824), 21, quoted by W. E. Sedgwick, *op. cit.*, p. 143.

[29] J. F. Cooper, *Notions of the Americans: Picked up by a Travelling Bachelor* (London, 1828), II, 142, quoted *idem*, pp. 142–143, note 5.

[30] *Idem*, II, 143.

[31] Irving to Mrs. Sarah Storrow, Honesdale, July 31, 1841; see his *Letters from Sunnyside and Spain*, ed. S. T. Williams (New Haven, London, 1928), p. 29.

[32] "Domestic Literature," *Atlantic Magazine*, I (June, 1824), 133, quoted in W. E. Sedgwick, *op. cit.*, p. 150.

33 The moral quality of supernatural tales was continually scrutinized. In American reviews of stories or of poems of the "Satanic School," the ethics of robbers and outlaws were also tested in the belief that the deeds of bandits must not be allowed to corrupt virtue. See William Charvat, *op. cit.*, pp. 69–71.

34 It is difficult to believe that the elaborate Gothic plot in *The House of the Seven Gables* is wholly free from satire.

35 "Modern Literature," *Atlantic Magazine*, I (May, 1824), 21–22, quoted by W. E. Sedgwick, *op. cit.*, pp. 144–145.

36 John Bristed, *America and Her Resources* (London, 1818), p. 356, quoted in *idem*, p. 147. Cf. Washington Irving: "Our lofty mountains and stupendous cataracts awaken no poetical associations, and our majestic rivers roll their waters unheeded, because unsung." *Biographies and Miscellanies*, ed. P. M. Irving, [*Irving's Works.*] *Hudson Ed.* (New York [c1856]–1889), XVII, 161.

37 J. F. Cooper, *op. cit.*, II, 142, quoted by W. E. Sedgwick, *op. cit.*, p. 142, note 5.

38 J. A. Hillhouse, *op. cit.*, p. 31, quoted in *idem*, p. 158.

39 William Tudor, "An Address Delivered to the Phi Beta Kappa Society," *North American Review*, II (November, 1815), 13–32, quoted in *idem*, p. 149.

40 See, in the present work, pp. 62–64.

41 "The more conservative critics clung to their Augustan rules; the more liberal ones were conscious of the need for new dictional technique but disliked some of the new English theory and practice. Wordsworth's theory came too early. In 1800 the world was not quite ready for it, and as a result it aroused an unreasoning prejudice which continued long after the world had become used to its practice in poetry. The more subjective and individualistic romantic poets, meanwhile, were experimenting with new connotations and shadings which seemed merely obscure to the many critics who were not developing with the new poetry." William Charvat, *op. cit.*, p. [86]. For a discussion of the reflection of the new theories in criticism, see *idem*, Chap. V.

42 One preface by Percival is especially important. See in the present chapter, p. 75.

43 Poe was an exception. He reviewed it severely in the *Southern Literary Messenger*, II (April, 1836), 326–336.

44 Reminiscence by Halleck's friend and correspondent, Mrs. Rush of Philadelphia, as quoted in J. G. Wilson, *The Life and Letters of Fitz-Greene Halleck* (New York, 1869), p. 305.

45 N. F. Adkins, *Fitz-Greene Halleck . . .* (New Haven, London, 1930), p. 200.

46 *Idem*, p. 199.

47 *Ibid.*

48 *Ibid.*

49

> I wandered through the lofty halls
> Trod by the Percys of old fame,
> And traced upon the chapel walls
> Each high, heroic name.

"Alnwick Castle," *The Poetical Writings of Fitz-Greene Halleck*, ed. J. G. Wilson (New York, 1869), p. 20.

[50] "On the Death of Joseph Rodman Drake, of New York, September, 1820," *idem*, pp. 34–35. This poem, printed in many anthologies, is the best-known of all Halleck's lyrics.

[51] "The American Flag," F. L. Pleadwell, ed., *The Life and Works of Joseph Rodman Drake* (Boston, 1935), p. 187.

[52] "Seneca Lake," *The Poetical Works of James Gates Percival* (Boston, 1859), II, 220.

[53] I do not agree with some recent critics who think that Poe was, after all, deeply concerned with religion and ethics.

[54] See, in the present work, pp. 84–85; 104.

[55] See "An Address Delivered before the Senior Class in Divinity College," *The Complete Works of Ralph Waldo Emerson*, ed. E. W. Emerson ([Boston and New York, 1903–04]), I, 122. The "moral" quality in the theory and practice of American poetry has, of course, been widely discussed. It expressed itself in hostility to Rousseau, Byron, and Goethe, to excessive individualism in social movements, to egotism of any kind. The attitudes against which the romantic poets slowly but surely made headway are reflected in the criticism of the period. "It subjected," says William Charvat, "all romantic poetry to the moral test." *Op. cit.*, p. [59]. See Chap. IV entire.

[56] Frederick Marryat, *A Diary in America* (London, 1839), II, 244.

[57] Although Percival's own treatment of his subjects was not exciting, this theory is startlingly in advance of his own time. See the Preface to his *Prometheus, Part II* (New-Haven, 1822) and William Charvat's discussion of a "free and careless style . . . the natural one for a dawning national literature." *Op. cit.*, pp. 100–101. This proleptic theory should be studied in the light of James Russell Lowell's attack on Percival.

[58] See *The Poetical Works of James Gates Percival*, *op. cit.*, I, 396–397.

[59] See E. A. Poe, "The Poetic Principle," *The Works of Edgar Allen Poe*, ed. E. C. Stedman and G. E. Woodberry (Chicago, 1894–95), VI, 8.

[60] These were: I, "On the Nature of Poetry"; II, "On the Value and Uses of Poetry"; III, "On Poetry in Its Relation to Our Age and Country"; IV, "On Originality and Imitation." See also Bryant's Introduction to *A New Library of Poetry and Song* (New York [c1876]), and his various critical essays. For brief summaries of his theories, see G. W. Allen, *American Prosody* (New York, Cincinnati [etc., c1935]), pp. 28–31, and H. H. Clark, *Major American Poets* (New York, Cincinnati [etc., c1936]), p. 797.

[61] R. H. Dana, "The Writer of the Idle Man, to His Old Friends," *Poems and Prose Writings* (Boston, 1833), p. 148.

[62] For the best summary of Wordsworth's influence upon American poetry, especially upon Bryant, see William Charvat, *op. cit.*, pp. 90–91. See also W. E. Leonard, *op. cit.*, pp. 42–44.

[63] "In the *Atlantic's* successor, the *New York Review and Atheneum Magazine*, which was edited by Bryant, the influence of Wordsworth is pervasive. One critic referred to neo-classical diction as 'The Cant of Poetry—a set of conventional phrases, formerly called poetic diction . . . now laid aside.'" William Charvat, *op. cit.*, p. 91.

[64] Lecture IV.

65 For an account of Bryant's early tastes in poetry, see Parke Godwin, *A Biography of William Cullen Bryant* (New York, 1883), I, 37.

66 Review of Solyman Brown, *An Essay on American Poetry*, in the *North American Review*, VII (July, 1818), 204.

67 *Ibid.*

68 See W. C. Bryant, *A New Library of Poetry and Song, op. cit.*, "Introduction," p. 13.

69 See William Charvat, *op. cit.*, Chap. III. Bryant was aware of Wordsworth but also of Burke, and he was in debt to Archibald Alison's *Essays on the Nature and Principles of Taste*. Although a transitional figure, Bryant's revolt from the Scottish thinkers was more striking than his allegiance to them.

70 "Lecture First. On the Nature of Poetry," *Prose Writings of William Cullen Bryant*, ed. Parke Godwin (New York, 1884), I, 10.

71 James Russell Lowell's phrase, quoted by Bryant. See *A New Library of Poetry and Song, op. cit.*, "Introduction," p. 12.

72 *Idem*, p. 11.

73 "The Poet," *The Poetical Works of William Cullen Bryant*, ed. Parke Godwin (New York, 1883), II, 135.

74 *A New Library of Poetry and Song, op. cit.*, "Introduction," p. 13.

75 See *ibid.*

76 See "Lecture Second. On the Value and Uses of Poetry," *Prose Writings of William Cullen Bryant, op. cit.*, I, 19.

77 For a summary of this element in his poetry, see *William Cullen Bryant, Representative Selections*, ed. Tremaine McDowell (New York, Cincinnati [etc., c1935]), pp. xlix–l.

78 See, in the present chapter, note 116.

79 Particularly in the poetry of the "Graveyard School." He said of his reading in boyhood: "I had, as young poets are apt to have, a liking for poetry of a querulous cast." See Parke Godwin, *op. cit.*, I, 37.

80 *New-York Mirror*, July 10, 1830. Quoted in *Minor Knickerbockers, op. cit.*, p. xlix. G. P. Morris praised Catharine Sedgwick's *Redwood* for "the pure spirit of morality which breathes through every page." *New-York Mirror*, June 26, 1824, quoted in *idem*, p. xlvii.

81 *Idem*, p. xlix. See also the entire section called "Literary Theories."

82 See "The Hurricane," *The Poetical Works of William Cullen Bryant, op. cit.*, I, 195–197; "To a Mosquito," *idem*, I, 153–156.

83 See "The Battle-Field," *idem*, I, 275–277, and "To the Fringed Gentian," *idem*, I, 221–222.

84 See "'I Broke the Spell that Held Me Long,'" *idem*, I, 99.

85 Herman Melville to Nathaniel Hawthorne. See Julian Hawthorne, *Nathaniel Hawthorne and His Wife* (Cambridge, 1884), I, 404.

86 "The Poet," *The Poetical Works of William Cullen Bryant, op. cit.*, II, 136.

87 An accusation first preferred, presumably, in Lowell's *A Fable for Critics*, *The Complete Poetical Works of James Russell Lowell*, Cambridge Ed. (Boston and New York [c1925]), pp. 131–132.

88 See, in the present work, pp. 81–82.

89 *The Poetical Works of William Cullen Bryant, op. cit.*, I, 144–145, 203–206.

[90] Bryant translated the Mexican poet, Moreno. For accounts of his associations with the Cuban poet, José María Heredia, see E. C. Hills, "Did Bryant Translate Heredia's Ode to Niagara?" *Modern Language Notes*, XXXIV (December, 1919), 503–505; Luciano de Acevedo, "Un Problema literario: Bryant tradujo la oda al Niagara, de Heredia?" *Cuba contemporánea*, XXII (February, 1920), 210–212; Emile Boxham, "El Gran poéta José María Heredia," *Cuba contemporánea*, XLI (June, 1926), 113–133.

[91] See W. A. Bradley, *William Cullen Bryant* (New York, 1926), pp. 203–204.

[92] "To a Friend," F. L. Pleadwell, ed., *op. cit.*, pp. 194–195.

[93] *A Funeral Oration, Occasioned by the Death of Thomas Cole, Delivered before the National Academy of Design, New-York, May 4, 1848* (New-York, Philadelphia, 1848), p. 14. See also his poem, "To Cole, the Painter, Departing for Europe," *The Poetical Works of William Cullen Bryant, op. cit.*, I, 219:

> . . . . thy heart shall bear to Europe's strand
> A living image of our own bright land,
> Such as upon thy glorious canvas lies;
> Lone lakes—savannas where the bison roves—
> Rocks rich with summer garlands—solemn streams—
> Skies, where the desert eagle wheels and screams—
> Spring bloom and autumn blaze of boundless groves.

[94] *The Bryant Festival at "The Century"* (New York, 1865), p. 17, as quoted in *William Cullen Bryant, Representative Selections, op. cit.*, p. xxxv.

[95] *Ibid.*

[96] *Idem*, p. xxxiv.

[97] Norman Foerster, *Nature in American Literature* (New York, 1923), p. 10.

[98] See *William Cullen Bryant, Representative Selections, op. cit.*, Introduction, III, p. xxiii–xxxi.

[99] See Parke Godwin, *op. cit.*, II, 108–109.

[100] "Robert Dinsmore," *The Works of John Greenleaf Whittier, Standard Library Ed.* ([Boston and New York, 1892–94]), VI, 245.

[101] *Idem*, p. 246.

[102] Whittier's literary self-cultivation offers a vivid contrast to his lack of formal education.

[103] See his letter to Lucy Hooper, Boston, August 27, 1837, *The Works of John Greenleaf Whittier, op. cit.*, VIII, 213. In 1832 he wrote:

> The truth is, I love poetry, with a love as warm, as fervent, as sincere, as any of the more gifted worshippers at the temple of the Muses.—I consider its gift as something holy and above the fashion of the world.

J. A. Pollard, *John Greenleaf Whittier, Friend of Man* (Boston, 1949), p. 101.

[104] "The Tent on the Beach," *The Works of John Greenleaf Whittier, op. cit.*, IV, 230. See also his poem, "In Peace," *idem*, IV, 70:

> To paint, forgetful of the tricks of art,
> With pencil dipped alone in colors of the heart.

[105] "Mezzo Cammin," *The Works of Henry Wadsworth Longfellow*, ed. Samuel Longfellow (Boston and New York, 1896–1901), I, 234; "Prelude," *idem*,

I, 16; "The Day is Done," *idem*, I, 222; "The Arrow and the Song," *idem*, I, 234; "Milton," *idem*, III, 201; "The Poets," *idem*, III, 210.

106 "Prelude," *idem*, I, 16.

107 See *Kavanagh, idem*, VIII, 365–371.

108 "Michael Angelo: A Fragment," *idem*, VI, 167.

109 Although evidence concerning this attitude of Longfellow's is hardly needed, an amusing illustration occurs in his quotation, in spite of his pleasure in medieval prose romances, of Ascham's attacks on the bad morals in chivalry. See William Charvat, *op. cit.*, p. 65.

110 Longfellow's studies of foreign languages produced no theory. G. W. Allen notes a few entries in Longfellow's Journal which are connected with the art of expression. *Op. cit.*, p. 156.

111 "The Day is Done," *The Works of Henry Wadsworth Longfellow, op. cit.*, I, 222.

112 See *Clemencia, novela de costumbres por Fernán Caballero* (Madrid, 1902), "Carta á mi lector de las Batuecas," p. xxxii.

113 "The Building of the Ship," *The Works of Henry Wadsworth Longfellow, op. cit.*, I, 249.

114 From at least a dozen languages. For translation Longfellow developed a few loosely-phrased theories. See "Introductory Note" to "Translations," *idem*, VI, [177]–182.

115 "The Day is Done," *idem*, I, 223.

116 See Floyd Stovall, "Poe's Debt to Coleridge," University of Texas, *Studies in English*, X (1930), [70]–127. See also H. T. Baker, "Coleridge's Influence on Poe's Poetry," *Modern Language Notes*, XXV (March, 1910), 94–95. Poe was in debt to many English nineteenth century poets. See E. I. Wiltshire, "The Influence of Nineteenth Century English Poetry on the Poetical Works of Edgar Allan Poe," unpublished master's essay, Yale University, 1939. His resemblance to Keats is suggested by the parallel between "Lamia" and his "Sonnet—to Science." See H. E. Rollins, *Keats' Reputation in America to 1848, op. cit.*, pp. 83–84.

117 Floyd Stovall believes "Al Aaraaf" to be an allegorical representation of Poe's theory of poetry. See "An Interpretation of Poe's 'Al Aaraaf,' " University of Texas, *Studies in English*, IX (1929), [106]–133.

118 It may be said that Poe's fame as a poet really began with the publication of *The Raven*, in 1845.

119 "Under the Microscope," *The Complete Works of Algernon Charles Swinburne*, ed. Sir Edmund Gosse and T. J. Wise (London, New York, 1925–27), VI, 418.

120 Discussions of Poe's prosody are numerous. See, in particular, W. L. Werner, "Poe's Theories and Practice in Poetic Technique," *American Literature*, II (May, 1930), [157]–165. For his definition of poetry, see G. W. Allen, *op. cit.*, pp. 57–61.

121 See his attack on American provincialism in his review of Drake's *The Culprit Fay, Southern Literary Messenger, op. cit.*

122 Although he sometimes praised Bryant's poetry, he did not regard him as a poet of unusual powers; and his hostility to Longfellow is well known.

[123] See E. I. Wiltshire, *op. cit.*

[124] E.g., his tale, "William Wilson."

[125] See *Poe's Short Stories*, ed. Killis Campbell (New York [1937]), "Introduction," pp. xviii–xx.

[126] "The volume of his [Poe's] verse is so slight as to confine his claim to its quality, and its quality is, in general, hardly such as to place him very high up on the fairly populous slopes of Parnassus where there is more competition than he met with in his lifetime. Competition is fatal to Poe. His cue was distinctly to function outside of it, and he was wise to cultivate originality at any price." W. C. Brownell, "Poe," *American Prose Masters* (New York, 1929), p. 217. A much more severe criticism of Poe came from Henry James, but centered in his tales. See "Charles Baudelaire," *French Poets and Novelists* (London, 1914), p.60.

[127] The essentials of Poe's theories can always be summarized briefly. E.g., see their condensation in eleven lines in Norman Foerster, *American Criticism* (Boston, 1928), pp. 6–7.

[128] "The Philosophy of Composition," *The Works of Edgar Allan Poe, op. cit.*, VI, 37.

[129] W. K. Wimsatt, Jr., "Poe and the Mystery of Mary Rogers," *Publications of the Modern Language Association*, LVI (March, 1941), 230–248.

[130] "The Poetic Principle," *The Works of Edgar Allan Poe, op. cit.*, VI, 3.

[131] *Idem*, p. 4.

[132] He was, however, as said, a student of Newton. See Margaret Alterton, *Origins of Poe's Critical Theories* (Iowa City [1925]), pp. 146, 155–156.

[133] See *Edgar Allan Poe; Representative Selections*, ed. Margaret Alterton and Hardin Craig, *op. cit.*, Introduction.

[134] "Robert Dinsmore," *The Works of John Greenleaf Whittier, op. cit.*, VI, 248.

[135] "The Poetic Principle," *The Works of Edgar Allan Poe, op. cit.*, VI, 12.

[136] *Idem*, VI, 28.

[137] See C. P. Cambiaire, *The Influence of Edgar Allan Poe in France* (New York, 1927), pp. 87–90; [95]–119; [120]–126.

[138] See *idem*, pp. 84–87, for references to statements by French critics which illustrate Poe's influence on the Parnassian School.

[139] W. B. Yeats, in a letter read at the celebration of the Poe centenary at the University of Virginia. See C. W. Kent and J. S. Patton, *The Book of the Poe Centenary* ([Charlottesville, Va.] 1909), p. 207.

[140] "The originality of his genius lay in the fact that he consciously attempted to amalgamate theory and practice in definite and specific instances." *Edgar Allan Poe, op. cit.*, p. xv.

[141] See "The Philosophy of Composition," *The Works of Edgar Allan Poe, op. cit.*, VI, 39. Note also Poe's continual use of prosodic devices which he had discussed in theory, such as the repetend.

[142] Poe's sardonic temper is evident in such a poem as "The Conqueror Worm," *The Poems of Edgar Allan Poe*, ed. Killis Campbell (Boston, New York [etc., c1917]), pp. 105–106.

[143] See P. E. More, "The Origins of Hawthorne and Poe," *Shelburne Essays . . . First Series* (New York and London, 1904), pp. 51–70.

[144] For illustrations, see G. W. Allen, *op. cit.*, pp. 63–85.

[145] See "The Rationale of Verse," *The Works of Edgar Allan Poe, op. cit.*, VI, 47–104.

[146] Theodore Watts-Dunton, "Poetry," *The Encyclopædia Britannica;* 11th ed. (Cambridge, Eng., New York, 1910–11), XXI, 880.

[147] Mrs. Browning to Poe, 5 Wimpole St., April, 1846. See G. E. Woodberry, "Poe in New York," *Century Illustrated Monthly Magazine*, XLVIII (October, 1894), 859.

[148] "Eldorado," *The Poems of Edgar Allan Poe, op. cit.*, p. 129.

[149] See W. D. Howells, *Literary Friends and Acquaintances* (New York and London, 1900), p. 63.

[150] "Ulalume," *The Poems of Edgar Allan Poe, op. cit.*, p. 119.

[151] "Eldorado," *idem*, p. 129.

[152] "Annabel Lee," *idem*, p. 135.

[153] "The City in the Sea," *idem*, p. 60–61.

[154] "Marginalia," *The Works of Edgar Allan Poe, op. cit.*, VII, 310.

[155] *Ibid.*

[156] Quoted by A. E. Housman, *The Name and Nature of Poetry* (New York, Cambridge, England, 1933), p. 36.

CHAPTER IV: THE POET OF PHILOSOPHIC THOUGHT

[1] For text and criticism see Perry Miller, *The Transcendentalists* . . . (Cambridge, Mass., 1950).

[2] For a discussion of the romantic elements in transcendentalist poetry, see Charles Cestre, "Le Romantisme d'Emerson," *Revue anglo-américaine*, VII (October, December, 1929), 1–18; [113]–131. Norman Foerster, however, believes that "the main current of Emerson's mind was not the romantic but the classic." *American Criticism* (Boston and New York, 1928), p. 84. See also J. S. Harrison, *The Teachers of Emerson* (New York, 1910).

[3] "The Poet," *The Complete Works of Ralph Waldo Emerson*, ed. E. W. Emerson ([Boston and New York, 1903–04]), III, 8. Hereafter referred to in this chapter as *Works*.

[4] T. W. Higginson, "The Sunny Side of the Transcendental Period," *Atlantic Monthly*, XCIII (January, 1904), 7, 13. Quoted by Elsie F. Brickett, "Studies in the Poets and Poetry of New England Transcendentalism,"unpublished dissertation, Yale University, 1937. To this work I am indebted for general assistance and for guidance to particular quotations; it will prove indispensable to future students of this literary movement. See especially its references in notes and bibliographies to writings concerning the transcendentalists.

[5] *Journals of Ralph Waldo Emerson*, ed. E. W. Emerson and W. E. Forbes (Boston and New York, 1909–14), May 24, 1847, VII, 279. Hereafter referred to in this chapter as *Journals*.

6 The least characteristic of these forms among the transcendentalists was the novel. Yet see Sylvester Judd, *Margaret. A Tale of the Real and Ideal, Blight and Bloom* (Boston, New York [etc.] 1845).

7 'See B. V. Thomas, "Osman in America: Emerson's Contemporary Reputation as a Poet, 1846–1882," unpublished master's essay, Yale University, 1930, p. 55.

8 See *Biographia Literaria* (Oxford, 1907), I, 164-166.

9 "The Transcendentalist," *Works*, I, [329].

10 *Ibid.*

11 For evidence of the importance of *Nature* in the development of transcendentalism, see E. F. Brickett, *op. cit.*, p. 5, note 1.

12 "The Transcendentalist," *Works*, I, [329].

13 Henry James, *Hawthorne* (New York, 1899), p. 81, as quoted by E. F. Brickett, *op. cit.*, p. 7, note 1.

14 "Self-Reliance," *Works*, II, 54.

15 "An Address Delivered before the Senior Class in Divinity College," *idem*, I, 145.

16 Transcendentalism was in debt to Puritanism for moral idealism, but it repudiated dogma.

17 E. F. Brickett, *op. cit.*, p. 6.

18 *The Poems of Emily Dickinson*, ed. M. D. Bianchi and A. L. Hampson (Boston, 1937), p. 163.

19 *The Correspondence of Thomas Carlyle and Ralph Waldo Emerson*, ed. C. E. Norton (Boston, 1883), I, 308.

20 "Threnody," *Works*, IX, 156.

21 See "The Poet," *idem*, III, 8.

22 "The World-Soul," *idem*, IX, 17.

23 "The Problem," *idem*, IX, 8.

24 See, in the present work, p. 14.

25 See N. F. Adkins, "Emerson and the Bardic Tradition," *Publications of the Modern Language Association*, LXIII (June, 1948), 667–669.

26 See, in the present chapter, p. 111.

27 "Walden," *The Writings of Henry David Thoreau*, [*Walden Ed.*] (Boston and New York [1906]), II, 279.

28 *Journal*, August 28, 1841, *idem*, VII, 275.

29 "A Week on the Concord and Merrimack Rivers," *idem*, I, 94.

30 Carl Bode's excellent edition, *The Portable Thoreau* (New York, 1947), reveals how slight, after all, was the body of his verse. See the discussion of his poetry in E. F. Brickett, *op. cit.*, Chap. IV. See also the quotation from Foerster, *idem*, p. 165, note 1.

31 "Thoreau," *Works* X, 474.

32 See, in the present chapter, p. 119.

33 *Journal*, August 28, 1841, *The Writings of Henry David Thoreau*, *op. cit.*, VII, 275.

34 "A Week on the Concord and Merrimack Rivers," *idem*, I, 313.

35 See E. F. Brickett, *op. cit.*, Chap. V., p. 230, note 1.

36 *Journals*, November 21, 1840, V, 494.

[37] Journal, March, 1838. Quoted by E. F. Brickett, *op. cit.*, p. 272.

[38] Journal, July, 1833. Quoted in *idem*, p. 253.

[39] Quoted in *idem*, p. 272.

[40] *Journals*, September, 1841, March 12, 1843, VI, 46, 358; September 20, 1846, VII, 230. See also *idem*, June 24, 1840, V, 417.

[41] Quoted from Emerson's "little manuscript book" of notes for a biography of Alcott, in F. B. Sanborn and W. T. Harris, *A. Bronson Alcott, His Life and Philosophy* (Boston, 1893), I, 346. See E. F. Brickett, *op. cit.*, p. 301, note 1.

[42] It should be remembered that all these poets, including Emerson, believed that to attain "inspiration" the poet must lead an abstemious life, renouncing all narcotics and stimulants. Whitman held similar views, though with less philosophical objectives. For the "favoring circumstances" important for the creation of poetry, see Jean Gorely, "Emerson's Theory of Poetry," *Poetry Review*, XXII (July-August, 1931), 267–268.

[43] See E. F. Brickett, *op. cit.*, Chap. III.

[44] Quoted in *idem*, p. 104, from *Memoirs of Margaret Fuller Ossoli*, ed. R. W. Emerson, W. H. Channing, J. F. Clarke, *Works* (Boston, 1874), I, 121.

[45] M. F. Ossoli, "American Literature," *Art, Literature, and the Drama*, ed. A. B. Fuller, *idem*, V, 308.

[46] "Questionings," *The Poets of Transcendentalism, an Anthology*, ed. G. W. Cooke (Boston and New York, 1903), p. 116.

[47] *Idem*, p. 84.

[48] "The Light from Within," *Poems and Essays by Jones Very* (Boston and New York, 1886), p. 174.

[49] In "The Poet," as a center, with other essays, poems, and the *Journals* with subsidiary material.

[50] "Initial, Dæmonic and Celestial Love," *Works*, IX, 115.

[51] See also *The Poets of Transcendentalism, op. cit.*

[52] C. P. Cranch, *Poems* (Philadelphia, 1844), p. 51.

[53] W. E. Channing, "A Poet's Hope," *Poems* (Boston, 1843), p. 100.

[54] E. g.:

> Who rides a beetle, which he calls a "Sphinx."
> And O what questions asked in club-foot rhyme
> Of Earth the tongueless and the deaf-mute Time!
> Here babbling "Insight" shouts in Nature's ears
> His last conundrum on the orbs and spheres;
> There Self-inspection sucks its little thumb,
> With "Whence am I?" and "Wherefore did I come?"

"An After-Dinner Poem," *The Poetical Works of Oliver Wendell Holmes* (Boston, 1881), I, 155.

[55] "Nature," *Works*, I, [3].

[56] See Norman Foerster, *American Criticism, op. cit.*, p. 52.

[57] For a discussion of Channing's dedication of his life to poetry, see E. F. Brickett, *op. cit.*, Chap. VI.

[58] *Journals*, December 18, 1841, VI, 144. Quoted by E. F. Brickett, *op. cit.*, p. 58.

⁵⁹ See his letter to Lydia Jackson, Concord, Feb. 1, 1835, *The Letters of Ralph Waldo Emerson*, ed. R. L. Rusk (New York, 1939), I, 435, See also *Journals*, August 23, 1820, May 7, 1822, I, 32, 137–138; May 15, 1827, II, 203; October 24, 1840, V, 481; December, 1862, IX, 472. Emerson published only two volumes of verse during his lifetime: *Poems* (1846) and *May-Day and Other Pieces* (1867). For an account of his poetry in the perspective of his entire career, see R. L. Rusk, *The Life of Ralph Waldo Emerson* (New York, 1949), pp. 312–323; 433–434.

⁶⁰ W. C. Brownell, "Emerson," *American Prose Masters* (New York, 1929), p. 189.

⁶¹ "Merlin," *Works*, IX, [120].

⁶² *A Correspondence between John Sterling and Ralph Waldo Emerson* (Boston and New York, 1897), p. 30. Quoted by E. F. Brickett, *op. cit.*, p. 57.

⁶³ "The Poet," *Works*, III, 26.

⁶⁴ *Journals*, December 9, 1868, X, 267.

⁶⁵ *Letters of James Russell Lowell*, ed. C. E. Norton (New York, 1894), II, 275. See also F. B. Sanborn, *The Genius and Character of Emerson* (Boston, 1885), p. 211.

⁶⁶ "Natural History of Intellect," *Works*, XII, 52–53. Quoted by E. G. Sutcliffe, *Emerson's Theories of Literary Expression* ([Urbana, 1923]), p. 122.

⁶⁷ *Journals*, May, 1854, VIII, 463.

⁶⁸ *Journals*, June 13, 1838, IV, 476.

⁶⁹ "The Poet," *Works*, III, 16, 30.

⁷⁰ *Idem*, p. 29.

⁷¹ "Bacchus," *idem*, IX, [125].

⁷² *Idem*, IX, 24.

⁷³ *Journals*, March 24, 1846, VII, 164.

⁷⁴ Besides the incidental definitions and comments, the student should examine "The Poet," "Poetry and Imagination," "Eloquence," "The Superlative," "Art and Criticism," and "Inspiration."

⁷⁵ See *Journals*, October 15, 1844, VI, 537, and October, 1820, I, [63]–65. Referred to by E. F. Brickett, *op. cit.*, p. 61.

⁷⁶ For a synthesis, see F. T. Thompson, "Emerson's Theory and Practice of Poetry," *Publications of the Modern Language Association, XLIII* (December, 1928), pp. 1170–1184.

⁷⁷ These two passages begin: "Crossing a bare common," *Works*, I, 9, and "Words are signs of natural facts," *idem*, p. [25].

⁷⁸ *Idem*, IX, 252.

⁷⁹ See *ante*, p. 99.

⁸⁰ *Works, IX*, 311.

⁸¹ *Idem*, IX, [120].

⁸² "Who stands astonished at the meteor light," "The Adirondacs," *idem*, IX, 186; "The light wherewith all planets shone," "Fragments on the Poet and the Poetic Gift," *idem*, p. 324; "Holds in check the frolic light," "Solution," *idem*, p. 222, etc.

⁸³ See *ante*, p. 106, note 77.

⁸⁴ *Works*, I, 9.

[85] See, in particular, for the influence of Neoplatonism in "The Poet," F. I. Carpenter, *Emerson and Asia* (Cambridge, 1930), pp. 86–94.

[86] "Art," *Works*, II, 352.

[87] "We denote this primary wisdom as Intuition, whilst all later teachings are tuitions. In that deep force, the last fact behind which analysis cannot go, all things find their common origin." "Self-Reliance," *idem*, II, 64.

[88] *Journals*, December (?), 1852, VIII, 353.

[89] See *ante*, p. 107, note 86.

[90] "The Poet," *Works*, IX, 312.

[91] "The Poet," *idem*, III, 5.

[92] John Morley, *Critical Miscellanies* (London and New York, 1888), I, 321.

[93] "Nature," *Works*, I, 76. See also "Swedenborg; or, The Mystic," *idem*, IV, 105, 120, etc. This idea of "currents" Emerson applies specifically to the poet: "The ethereal tides ... roll and circulate through him; then he is caught up into the life of the Universe." "The Poet," *idem*, III, 26.

[94] "The Poet," *idem*, III, 8–9.

[95] See *Journals*, January 12, 1822, I, 106.

[96] *Idem*, 1876, X, 464.

[97] "The Poet," *Works*, III, 37.

[98] "Initial, Dæmonic and Celestial Love," *idem*, IX, 115.

[99] "Nature," *idem*, I, [25].

[100] *Ibid.*

[101] *Idem*, p. 4.

[102] "The American Scholar," *idem*, I, 111. Any symbol will do to interpret any divine element in Nature: "In the transmission of the heavenly waters, every hose fits every hydrant." "Swedenborg; or, The Mystic," *idem*, IV, 121.

[103] See the excellent summary of the ideas underlying Emerson's dualism in *Ralph Waldo Emerson, Representative Selections*, ed. F. I. Carpenter (New York, Cincinnati [etc., c1934]), pp. xxx–xxxviii.

[104] "Fragments on the Poet and the Poetic Gift," *Works*, IX, 325. Quoted by E. F. Brickett, *op. cit.*, p. 60.

[105] "The Sphinx," *Works*, IX, 22.

[106] "The Sphinx," *idem*, IX, 21.

[107] "Europe and European Books," *idem*, XII, 366.

[108] The student should note how many "natural facts" are cited in the poem "Each and All," *idem*, IX, 4–6. For a discussion of the relationship of the concrete and the abstract in Emerson's thought, see *Ralph Waldo Emerson, Representative Selections*, *op. cit.*, p. xxxiii. These "natural facts" appear endlessly in the poetry. E. g.:

> Each chimney-pot and cottage door,
> Farm-gear and village picket-fence.

"The Poet," *Works*, IX, 311.

> Give to barrows, trays and pans
> Grace and glimmer of romance.

"Art," *idem*, IX, 277.

[109] "The Poet," *idem*, III, 24.

[110] "The Sphinx," *idem*, IX, 22.

[111] *Journals*, September 27, 1836, IV, 102. See, in contrast, Poe's definition, in the present work, p. 88.

[112] *Journals*, June 21, 1835, III, 492.

[113] *Idem*, November 13, 1841, VI, 124.

[114] See the discussion of Emerson's practice in the present chapter, p. 119.

[115] "Poetry and Imagination," *Works*, VIII, 29.

[116] "The Poet," *idem*, III, 10.

[117] "The Poet," *ibid.*

[118] "The Study of Poetry," *The Works of Matthew Arnold* ([London, 1903–04]), IV, 1.

[119] "The Poet," *Works*, III, 9–10.

[120] *Journals*, October 19, 1842, VI, 286; "The Poet," *Works*, III, 9.

[121] "Merlin," *idem*, IX, [120].

[122] "The Poet," *idem*, III, 9.

[123] *Journals*, September 4, 1857, IX, 114.

[124] "The Poet," *Works*, III, 8.

[125] "Country Life," *idem*, XII, 157.

[126] "The Problem," *idem*, IX, 6–7.

[127] "Merlin," *idem*, IX, [120].

[128] *Journals*, November 13, 1841, VI, 124.

[129] This passage is quoted by Norman Foerster in connection with a discussion of this "organic" poetry. *Op. cit.*, p. 63. See also his article, "Emerson on the Organic Principle in Art," *Publications of the Modern Language Association*, XLI (March, 1926), 194: "He takes the objects of nature, any objects of nature, unfixes them, 'makes them revolve around the axis of his primary thought, and disposes them anew.' That is the 'creation of beauty.' "

[130] Emerson's phrases concerning the sentences of Montaigne. See "Montaigne; or, The Skeptic," *Works*, IV, 168.

[131] See "The Poet," *idem*, III, 17.

[132] *Journals*, June 24, 1840, V, 419.

[133] See *ante*, p. 111.

[134] "The Poet," *Works*, III, 17. "The transcendentalist worships the symbol. He believes that the writer's principal power is the effective use of figures of speech." E. G. Sutcliffe, *op. cit.*, p. 17.

[135] "The Poet," *Works*, III, 20. One of Emerson's favorite examples of the organic poet, of the true symbolist, is Shakespeare. See "Shakspeare; or, The Poet," *idem*, IV, 213–218.

[136] The Puritan poets were natural symbolists. See, in the present work, p. 20.

[137] See *ante*, p. 108.

[138] See, in the present work, p. 93.

[139] *Journals*, June 30, 1826, II, 109; quoted by F. T. Thompson, "Emerson's Theory and Practice of Poetry," *Publications of the Modern Language Association*, *op. cit.*, p. 1172.

[140] See J. B. Moore, "Emerson on Wordsworth," *idem*, XLI (March, 1926), 191.

[141] See S. T. Coleridge, *op. cit.*, I, 202.

[142] "Self-Reliance," *Works*, II, 51.

[143] See, in the present work, p. 110.

[144] "My Garden," *Works*, IX, 231.

[145] *Journals*, September, 1845, VII, 92.

[146] "Days," *Works*, IX, 228.

[147] "Art," *idem*, VII, 45.

[148] See *ante*, p. 105.

[149] "The Problem," *Works*, IX, 8.

[150] "Monadnoc," *idem*, IX, 65. See also the poem called "The World-Soul," *idem*, pp. 15–19.

[151] "Each and All," *idem*, IX, 6.

[152] *Journals*, 1852, VIII, 273–274.

[153] *Works*, IX, [248].

[154] "Emerson the Lecturer," *The Writings of James Russell Lowell*, [*Riverside Ed.*] ([Boston and New York, 1892]), I, 354.

[155] Emerson's theory of "involuntary" language included use of the contemporary world, such as the city, the railway, the factory. Thus he appears to have anticipated Jeffers, Sandburg, and Hart Crane in sanctioning for poetry these elements in American industrial life just as he seems to anticipate Robert Frost in authentic transcripts of American rural life. Actually, he himself made little use of such materials. See, however, the poems, "The World-Soul" and "The Adirondacs," *Works*, IX ,15–19, [182]–194. See "The Poet," *idem*, III, 19, and 37–38, and "Poetry and Imagination," *idem*, VIII, 37. See also "Music," *idem*, IX, [365]:

> But in the mud and scum of things
> There alway, alway something sings.

[156] "Initial, Dæmonic, and Celestial Love," *idem*, IX, 115–117.

[157] *A Concordance to the Poems of Ralph Waldo Emerson*, by G. S. Hubbell (New York, 1932), lists more than seventy references to "Time" (p. 419) and twenty-three to "Forms" (p. 146).

[158] "The Bohemian Hymn," *Works*, IX, [359].

[159] *Idem*, IX, 21.

[160] "Ode to Beauty," *idem*, IX, 89.

[161] "Initial, Dæmonic, and Celestial Love," *idem*, IX, 110.

[162] "Uriel," *idem*, IX, 14.

[163] "The Bohemian Hymn," *idem*, IX, [359].

[164] We now know that he derived much of his material from secondary sources. See B. J. Whiting, "Emerson, Chaucer, and Thomas Warton," *American Literature*, XVII (March, 1945), [75]–78.

[165] His unwillingness to learn languages is well-known. He was content with translations.

[166] "The American Scholar," *Works*, I, 89.

[167] *Idem*, IX, [242].

[168]
> Or Music pours on mortals
> Its beautiful disdain.
> "World-Soul," *idem*, IX, 16.

[169] "Initial, Dæmonic, and Celestial Love," *idem*, IX, 115.

[170] See *Much Ado About Nothing*, Act III, scene i, line 7.

[171] See A. E. Bestor, Jr., "Emerson's Adaptation of a Line from Spenser," *Modern Language Notes*, XLIX (April, 1934), 265–267.

[172] *Journals*, August 10, 1838, V, 12.

[173] *Idem*, May 25, 1837, IV, 246.

[174] See in the present chapter, pp. 118, 122.

[175] "Merlin," *Works*, IX, [120]. Cf. *ante*, p. 112.

[176] See Vivian C. Hopkins, *Spires of Form, a Study of Emerson's Aesthetic Theory* (Cambridge, 1951), p. 115.

[177] For a discussion of Emerson's reading in the seventeenth century, see N. A. Brittin, "Emerson and the Metaphysical Poets," *American Literature*, VIII (March, 1936), [1]–21.

[178] "Literature," *Works*, V, 255.

[179] "Shakspeare; or, The Poet," *idem*, IV, 217.

[180] "It is the necessity of my nature to shed all influences. Who can come near to Kehama? Neither the rain, neither the warm ray of love, nor the touch of human hand." *Journals*, December 22, 1839, V, 355.

[181] "The Poet," *Works*, III, 18.

[182] "Hamatreya," *idem*, IX, [35]. He liked "the mere collection of meteoric particles, since the ability to create astronomic systems or even constellations was denied him." E. G. Sutcliffe, *op. cit.*, p. 124.

[183] Cf. *ante*, p. 111.

[184] "Days" might be said to be made up of a "sestet" and "quintet." Theoretically again, Emerson had no interest in the traditional forms as such.

[185] For an illuminating discussion of Emerson's rhymes, structures, and other techniques, see O. W. Firkins, *Ralph Waldo Emerson* (Boston and New York, 1915), Chap. VI.

[186] "Ode Inscribed to W. H. Channing," *Works*, IX, [76]–77.

[187] For Emerson's use of blank verse, heroic couplets, octosyllabics, etc., see G. W. Allen, *American Prosody* (New York, Cincinnati [etc., c1935]), pp. 96–118.

[188] "Ode Sung in the Town Hall, Concord, July 4, 1857," *Works*, IX, [199].

[189] See, in the present work, pp. 65–72.

[190] *Works*, IX, [248].

[191] "An Address Delivered before the Senior Class in Divinity College," *idem*, I, [119].

[192] "Nature," *idem*, I, 16.

[193] "The Snow-Storm," *idem*, IX, [41]–42.

[194] Cf. *ante*, p. 111.

[195] "The Snow-Storm," *Works*, IX, 42.

[196] "Merlin," *idem*, IX, 121.

[197] See *ante*, p. 112.

[198] Compare this passage ("The Poet," *Works*, III, 37) with the preface to the 1855 edition of Whitman's *Leaves of Grass*, ed. Emory Holloway (Garden City, New York, 1931), pp. 490–491, etc.